Ba Ha Ha Ha

Bahaha
Happy!

By Robyna Smith-Keys

Revised 13th November 2012

Revised 20th April 2014

Edition 5 Created March 2016

i

By Robyna Smith-Keys.

COPYRIGHT PAGE

ISBN: 978-0-9945693-1-8

ISBN-13: 978-0-9945693-1-8

(Robyna Smith-Keys of Beauty School Books)

ISBN-10: 0994569319

Published April 2016 by Beauty School Books

http://www.beautyschoolbooks.com

Ba Ha Ha Happy!

Copyright Key Points: Certain material is automatically protected by copyright under Australian law. There is no Registration of copyright in Australia, and no formal procedures to go through.

Copyright gives its owner the legal right to take action in certain circumstances if someone else uses their material. Criminal proceedings can be brought. In some circumstances, copyright owners can rely on presumptions that they own copyright, rather than having to prove ownership.

In addition to copyright, both technological protection measures and contractual terms can be used to limit other people ability to have access to or use copyright material.

By Robyna Smith-Keys.

Table Of Contents

By Robyna Smith-Keys.

Contained here in these pages we are going to practice being marvelously alive. The merry-go-round of life is a very giddy ride. It is a rollercoaster of ups, downs and round and around.

When you are tense or depressed, you are sick and your thinking's clouded. You need to know when to get of.

So where is off, you might ask. Well off is in your mind. Stop the merry-go-round in your mind. What you cannot fix needs to be - dealt with, mentally or you will stay on the merry-go-round.

in the world of thought, all the **"what ifs"**. All the **"if I had done"** thoughts, will not fix **"what is"**.

What is.

By Robyna Smith-Keys.

Is what it is.

They are who they are. You are who you are. The situation is what it is.

All you can control is your mind.

So lets get to it.

Lets control the most controllable part of your life.

Your Mind.

The feeling of being marvelously alive is a journey of three steps forward and two steps back. Will you ever take three steps forward and stay there happy and contented every single moment of every single day for the rest of your life. No! Sorry!... Everyone we know and everyone we are associated with will add either joy or dismay to our journey. But, you can learn to control the merry-go -round of life. You can learn to have more control and increase your moments of joy.

2

"*L*ife is not measured by the number of breaths we take, but by the moments that take our breath away."

- Unknown.

The world is spinning; At Earth's equator, the speed of Earth's spin is about 1,000 miles per hour (1,600 kph). The day-night has carried you around in a grand circle under the stars every day of your life, and yet you don't feel Earth spinning. Why not? It's because you and everything else – including Earth's oceans and atmosphere – are spinning along with the Earth at the same constant speed.

You have a motor and an energy field. Consequently, when you are upset you cannot think straight. When you give into negative thought patterns, your motor breaks down and will prevent you from, functioning, effectively.

3

By Robyna Smith-Keys.

Just like a car or a merry-go-round. You cannot stay in your car or on the merry-go-round all day. The car and the merry-go-round need repairs, oil, water and fuel. You need to get about so you do not feel stiff. Affirmation, meditation, self-talk, laughter and many other positive actions need to become part of your daily maintenance and sustenance.

LAUGHTER

If you want to make god laugh,
tell him about your plans.

- Woody Allen

~~ *** ~~

Buddha once said;-

He that learns to laugh at him-self is the wealthiest
of men. For he will have, endless amusement.

~~ *** ~~

"Laugh, and the world laughs with you;
weep, and you weep alone".

- Ella Wheeler Wilcox

~~ *** ~~

Everyone could fill a book on how important
laughter is. Laughter is good for your health.
Laughter relaxes the whole body. A good,

By Robyna Smith-Keys.

hearty laugh relieves physical tension and stress, leaving your muscles relaxed for up to 45 minutes after and laughter boosts the immune system.

It is hard to find a way to laugh when you are depressed.

Laughter Yoga combines unconditional laughter with yogic breathing (Pranayama). Anyone can laugh for no reason, without relying on humor, jokes or comedy. Laughter is simulated as a body exercise in a group but with eye contact and childlike playfulness, it soon turns into real and contagious laughter.

The concept of Laughter Yoga, is based on a scientific fact that the body cannot differentiate between fake and real laughter. One gets the same physiological and psychological benefits from a fake laugh and a real laugh.

Have a look at this website:-

Ba Ha Ha Happy!

http://www.laughteryoga-australia.org/about-laughteryoga.html

There are also laughter videos on YouTube.

By a daily practice of laughing, sooner than you think you will embrace the joy

of a hearty laugh.

EMOTIONAL STABILITY.

What each of us needs to be taught is how to like our self when others express their dislike for us. How to stay completely detached from the bitterness in other peoples expressions of us. How, to still see and enjoy the beauty in a person, when they are cruel to us. Their spite is not really about you. It is a reflection of their shortcomings. Their inability - to understand, the complex nature of the human mind.

By Robyna Smith-Keys.

The mind is very complicated made up from loads of different happening, sufferings and circumstances.

We can never ever know what has gone into the raveling that has made up a personality of another person.

Therefore, it stands to reason, that we should not be trying to sort through who we can enjoy and who we should avoid to have a happy life. We ought to be learning to stay calm, considerate, understanding, loving and helpful, when all odds are against us doing so; in the company of some people.

When someone attacks our equilibrium, we need to learn, to stay calm and non-abusive.

When someone makes a statement about us that is upsetting we need to be understanding - that it is the raveling composition of their mind that has caused them to feel the way they do, by something we said or did. It can often be what they think we said or did, when in actual- fact we did not do anything nor say anything remotely like what they are accusing us of.

You cannot stop a charging bull; all you can do is, run like hell for safety.

An alcoholic or drug addict: is a nightmare to live with. They are fanatical about their habit.

"*A* fanatic is one who can't change his mind

and won't change the subject."

— Winston S. Churchill

A fanatic, a gossip or that someone that is upset with us, metaphorically is our charging bull. As is that - someone; that is jealous of you. They pronounce things about you, usually state these things in a text message or to others, behind your back. All you can do is ignore them and feel complimented! Do not defend yourself, dust their comments off and feel proud. Their audience will be either people that don't matter or those that see through them.

Instead of trying, to defend our-self by having a go back at them we need to detach our self from their statement. Instead of becoming hurt and feeling down, we need to learn to zip it. Push it out of our mind.

We may never get the chance to set them straight. Even if we get the chance, to set them straight it could fuel their fire or ravel their thinking patterns more.

Therefore, in exercising our defense, we are going to waste loads of valuable energy and time, feeling either depressed or suppressed.

Feelings have a life expectancy. How long you expect to feel incomplete is all up to you. On the other hand, symptoms such as anger, fear, jealousy, depression, sadness and so on all have cures.

Suffering is the refusal to accept:

"What is".

How long you suffer is all up to you. How much self-help work you do at feeling marvelously alive is all so entirely up to you and just you.

Healing is really just setting yourself free, accepting the things you cannot change and having the courage to change the things you can.

It's letting yourself filter and process what you had to suppress at the time to keep going, maybe even to survive.

As a child when I was upset about someone calling me names or expressing their incorrect thoughts of me, my mother would say:

By Robyna Smith-Keys.

"Sticks and stones may break my bones but names will never hurt me".

Mum would encourage me to chant this idiom and it did help somehow. Not that as a child I fully understood the profound, philosophical weight of this idiom.

There are positive thinking Verses and Affirmations in this book to prompt you into wishful and thought provoking thinking. If you do not intend to be happy, you are without hope.

So get started right now.

Work towards feeling marvelously alive.

Learn the amazing art of:

"AGREEING TO DISAGREE".

Head for cover when all else fails. "Zip It" close your mouth and say nothing. People that feel guilty will blame you to take the focus off them.

Their mind becomes so tangled they need to justify their guilt in their tangled web of a mind. They are like a pray mantis waiting for the opportunity to attack you. They also have a need to get people on their side. They will either make up stories about you or twist the truth about you.

Sick people will always enter in and out of your life. Some of them are family members.

All too often, there is nothing you can do about what they are thinking. There is nothing, you can do to stop their gossip nor their bad behavior.

What you can do; is not let it affect you.

By Robyna Smith-Keys.

Prove to yourself; you are character wealthy, by being of good character. Work on your-self worth day by day.

Meditate their thoughts away.

Dismiss their thoughts and actions and refuse to think about their words and thoughts.

If you feel their thoughts of you are twisted, you are probably right. They are not willing to debate the issue nor will they agree to disagree. You can have a senseless argument about the issue, which will leave you both traumatized with no results in view. The better options are:-

To zip it. Say Nothing.

Tell them you agree that they have a point of view and you accept that; but feel very differently to them about the issue.

Is all this easy?

Ba Ha Ha Happy!

No! It takes practice.

Affirmations;-you can make your own, find one in this book to suit the situation or Google your thoughts.

Read inspiring verses.

Meditate.

Have a heart to heart with yourself.

Ring Lifeline or some other free telephone counseling service.

Have a few sessions with a counselor, a psychologist, or a psychic.

Join a positive thinking group. Such as, Grow, AA, Al-Anon, Bible study, or any group that will help you on your journey to a more, healthy mind set.

By Robyna Smith-Keys.

Abusers try to make you feel guilty, shameful, and helpless, so they can control you, but deep within you is a voice that disagrees. At first, the voice is quite loud, but each session of abuse knocks it down a bit until finally you can barely hear it at all. It's time to start listening to your inner voice. The inner voice may say things like:

"How can you treat me like this?"

"I certainly didn't do anything wrong."

"I don't deserve this."

"I hate when he/she acts like this and treats me so appallingly."

Your feelings are also indicators of abuse. Feeling afraid, ashamed, belittled, ignored, dominated, or manipulated is like a giant, flashing, and warning lights with sirens that scream out, "This isn't right!"

They could be a narcissistic personality type, which means they are sick, they lack empathy. You cannot cure them; all you can do is cure you. In the mean time, send them healings. I have been trying to heal people in my life for over 60 years. To-date it has not worked.

However, positive thinking has helped me, to step out of their control. They no longer have any power over my life or my feelings. They no longer affect my feelings, for more than a few minutes to a few hours. One of them still tries to hurt me, but I never react nor respond, I cannot cure them, they are mentally unstable. I have faced the fact that they have been conditioned to see the worst in people. Now I send them healings with the hope that they will one day heal. Yes, it can be very painful; loving people that speak ill of you and treat you badly.

That is where the sane ones in our world help us with the art of unconditional love.

By Robyna Smith-Keys.

Meditation and self-talk has worked miracles for me, I pray it does for you as well. So there you have a fine example that no matter how much you wish or pray someone will improve they cannot. They are sick. All you can do is change your feelings and acceptance of others.

AFFIRMING HAPPINESS.

Positive Affirmations are powerful words made up from your conscious mind needs.

We all know what we need but far too often believe and accept the fact that we do not have what we want.

We think it is out of our reach. We continue through our life without filling our hearts with great joy.

When an affirmation is chanted, or spoken aloud, our need or want becomes a definite possibility.

We place a sustenance deposit in our unconscious mind. Like a wish. A goal, an ambition.

How often have you heard the phrase?

By Robyna Smith-Keys.

"Be careful what you wish for you just might get it".

Before placing sustenance in our mind be certain it does not involve another person in a controlling way. Be mindful of the fact that danger lurks at every corner of our mind.

Your future feelings of being marvelously alive must center on your own personal feelings and the development in strengthening your responses and reactions to your life patterns and emotions.

Affirmations deposit our wishes into our subconscious mind. Then without realizing it, we work at getting what we want. Our subconscious mind is our pantry where our sustenance is stored. Just as we need to have food in our kitchen pantry, we need to have sustenance in our minds pantry.

Ba Ha Ha Happy!

An affirmation psychology is a positive thought or statement affirming that a desired, goal / aspiration has been reached, or is within reach. A statement of our goals, hopes and dreams that we announce aloud. When we have a commonsense talk to our self aloud, we affirm our intensions as a result.

When things are drastically wrong in our life we must focus on the way we want it to be. Not, how our life actually is. We must affirm with our self, that our life is already the way we want things and situations to be.

We need more of all kinds of things in our life. We have not, been placed here on Earth to be miserable.

We are here to be tested.

We are here to learn lessons and the quicker we learn our lessons the more peaceful we will feel.

We are here to grow:-

By Robyna Smith-Keys.

First stage is growing physically.

Second stage is our mental growth.

Third stage is our spiritual growth.

Fourth stage is our peaceful growth

Firth stage is decaying gracefully.

Then we pass over.

As Gandhi once said,

"I very jealously guarded my character.

The least little blemish drew tears from my eyes".

Your daily affirmation should be:-

"I will very jealously guard my character. The smallest blemish will hinder my growth. Therefore, I will this day guard my morals and my character with thoughtful actions".

What I think Gandhi is telling us here, we must first strive to be of good character. Then we must guard our character by being in the best company and in the best places. When we are not in the best of company, we must know how to be of good character and walk away from the situation we have found-not to be part of who we are striving to be.

I love the fact that there is a vast difference between spending time with a true lady /gentleman and someone who has no social graces. Those with no social graces need our friendship more than those that have been groomed. Often throughout my life, I found the un-groomed (those with no social graces) are the ones that will very willingly help and expect nothing in return. It is important to have friends of many different character types. All people from all walks-of-life add very interesting flavours to our life. Everyone plays a role in whom we are and who/how we are becoming.

SENDING HEALINGS

A healing-can be sent to yourself or others. There is magic in believing. First, you must heal yourself and place a protective light around yourself. There are both bad and good forces that entice us. The bad forces of the world tempt us to be rude, angry, unjust, unfair, unreasonable, bad mouthed and many other forms of negative behavior. The goodliness forces tempt us to think before we speak or act, to do the right thing, say sorry when we fall short of our perfect behavior patterns.

We all must read as many books as we can on being of good character. We must learn and teach how to conduct our lives in a very pure lady / gentlemanly way. We must all question

Ba Ha Ha Happy!

our actions, thoughts and deeds and strive to be the best person we possibly can be.

HEAL YOURSELF.

Sit in a quiet place

Close our eyes

Center your heartbeat by breathing in deeply through your nose and releasing your breath slowly though your mouth.

Repeat the breathing until you feel calm.

Try to empty your head from any chaos you may be experiencing.

Visualize a white light that surrounds your entire body.

By Robyna Smith-Keys.

Visualize your Guardian Angel at your side. Everyone is given-a personal, Guardian Angel at birth.

Now visualize your negatives as devils. Each negative situation is a devil.

See these little devils leaving your body.

As they leave you, one-by-one see other Angels taking each devil by the hand and leading him away from you.

Say, out loud:-

Go! Go! Go!

See the devils carrying away things, people and illness you no longer need in your life.

Once you feel all that you need to rid yourself of has gone, feel at peace and breathe a sigh of relief.

Ba Ha Ha Happy!

Now visualize a circle of fire surrounding the outer edge of your aura of white light.

This is now sealing in your good health and your dreams.

Blow the fire out visually.

See yourself in this renewed state of health and free from your devils and the devils advocates.

Say:-

I am now in a healing state.

I am now a better person.

I am now in a fit state to handle and push negatives out of my life.

While taking long slow deep breathes, visualize a seal of white protective light around your entire body from the soles of your feet to the tip of your head.

Say:-

By Robyna Smith-Keys.

I am now clean and pure.

I will now experience true and pure positive feelings of healing.

I will now be on good terms with all and loved by many.

So Mote it be -Amen

POWER AND ATTRACTION

Mind Power is Greater Than You Think.

The power of the mind along with the Law of Attraction is very powerful when used correctly. You can use affirmation to attract all that you want and desire, all that you need and should have. You need to trust in the fact that if it is to be it will be. If you want it enough you will receive.

People that belong to a Church, or some other powerful association and attend a weekly meeting of their choice gather like-minded friends. The more people you associate with the more power you have in life. You know the old saying:-

"A friend in need is a friend in deed".

If you are mixing with people from all walks of life, the safer you feel when you need a service of some kind. If a Mechanic, Dentist, Doctor, Hairdresser and so on, goes to your group he/she is less likely to steer you in the wrong direction or do the wrong thing by you.

It does not need to be a Church, it can be Lions club or Rotary or some other group that concentrates on helping others. When people are striving to be the best person they can be they are by far the best people to have in your life.

For your life to become emotionally, stable you need to mix with people that lead a better life than you do. You need to put time aside to be part of a group, of like-minded people.

There is great power in numbers.

The more like-minded people, you mix with the greater your power to achieve will be.

However, the opposite is also a powerful series of events when you mix with people that are going nowhere and have no intension of going anywhere in life. They are all talk and no action. They also have wants and needs but, constantly set in place patterns that prevent them from reaching goals. They are- weighed down, with far too many bad habits.

During our life we will work through the patterns of our upbringing. What we all must do is work out which patterns have been thoughtfully designed and improved upon. Then, which patterns have formed from either the lack of inspirational guidance or a lack of careful instruction from our parents/ guardians.

Personally, we all have a complex nature. Each child receives the guidance a parent/guardian gives, to all their children, differently. Parents usually give the same instructions to each child at certain times.

They try to instill the same set of morals and manners in each child. Naturally, a parent does not speak the same way to a three year old as they do to their six year old. They may even have stronger rules for their teenage daughter than they do for their teenage son.

Your parents have done the best they could to shape you. It is all in accordance with the journey they have had through their life. All your childhood experiences shape you. As an adult, it is all up to you to shape and reshape your future.

By Robyna Smith-Keys.

No one can undo his or her past but you can design and shape your future. Most parents or guardians unintentionally produce a combination of children.

Staying motivated is <u>not</u> always easy. That is why we need to develop daily habits of self-improvement. There is no point in reading a book that empowers you today, unless you plan to stay empowered and set some goals. The goals must be worked on every single day for the rest of your life. Other self empowered people are also important to your growth. Unlike some folk, I do not believe we should rid our self of negative people, they need us and we need them. Everyone has worth.

We do need to tip the scale though. The scale of family and friends should be weighted down with positive, good-natured well-adjusted people.

Ba Ha Ha Happy!

It may help you to have compassion if you can remember these negative behaviors are projections of their own self-hatred and feelings of inadequacy. Their bad behavior has nothing to do with you.

WE HAVE THREE MINDS.

A Conscious Mind,

A Subconscious Mind

An Unconscious Mind.

Learning to develop our minds in an all-inspiring way is the key to many great happenings. Such as:- peace of mind, self worth, respect and admiration from others.

The most rewarding feeling from mind power is the wonderful feeling of self worth, without the need for approval from others.

By Robyna Smith-Keys.

Our thoughts begin in our conscious mind. Whatever we truly believe; will move into our subconscious mind.

The subconscious mind will accept anything that you feed to it and it will carry out your every wish.

So, whatever you consistently think about whether it is real or imagined your subconscious mind will accept it is as the truth and it will find a way to bring to you whatever it is that you desire. Good, Bad Or Evil doings.

Your subconscious mind along with Law of Attraction will see to it that you attract to yourself all things and circumstances. Thus will ensure you have what you believed you would have.

If you consistently tell yourself that you are broke and you do not have the money to go on vacation, buy a new car or purchase the home of your dreams, your subconscious mind will believe your words and those things will, be kept away from you.

You are what you think you are and your subconscious mind will act out your wishes.

Be mindful of what you are thinking and wishing for. What you truly want to come into your existence will come in time. Sometimes, it comes much quicker than you think.

See yourself with whatever it is that you want. Let that picture sink into your subconscious mind by picturing or saying exactly what you want continuously with feeling.

The main point I need to make here is; what you want cannot be a particular person unless they want you as well.

With the power of the mind, you can have whatever it is that you want. Naturally, you have to start working on the changes you need to make in your life. But, if you cannot change anything right now do not let that stop you from knowing you will eventually have what you want.

 Keep believing, you will live a life of luxury and you eventually will.

If you wish to be wealthy, create a mental picture; see yourself living in luxury, see yourself in the most expensive stores paying cash for the things that you like, living in the mansion of your dreams and driving the car that you would like to drive.

MIND PICTURES.

Create mental pictures in your mind.

Allow those pictures to sink into to your subconscious mind. Your subconscious mind, will determine your vibration and once you get emotionally involved in the images of what you want, you will be sending out strong vibrations into the universe.

With the "Law Of Attraction", you will attract to you, all the things that you need in order to act in accordance with the mental pictures. The pictures that you are feeding into your subconscious mind.

As you go through life figuring out what you want and do not want, your subconscious mind along with the Law of Attraction will make available the necessary avenues or ideas. These avenues and ideas even your dreams and hopes, are needed in order for you to attract to you all things that you desire into your life.

 If you want a house put a picture of a lovely house on your refrigerator door. If you want a campervan or a nice car put a photo of that car on the refrigerator door. If you want better health put photos of the food you should eat on the refrigerator door.

By Robyna Smith-Keys.

There will always be some things, which you cannot change, because of outside laws. You may need to learn how to accept those things and focus on what you can change to make people and situations more joyful.

You cannot change the weather, but you can move to where the weather patterns are more to your liking. If you cannot move to another town, learn to love your town you are in by getting more involved in your town.

Research ways to improve how you can better manage the climate where you live.

I love to write for several hours early each morning. A pretty garden is also important to me. When I moved to Queensland to cope with the heat I needed to change my daily habits. I now have a break from writing about 7.30 am to take care of my garden for an hour. You need to accept "what is" and work around every situation.

38

You cannot bring someone back from heaven but you can learn to enjoy the memory of him or her and the joy of their existence. Even if a child is stillborn, you have known the joy of pregnancy. Some women will never know the excitement or fears associated with being told they are going to have a baby. Nor will they ever form bonds with other expectant mothers.

It is a cruel world and the thing you fear most must be the things you surmount and conquer.

In brief to conquer our mind is the most powerful thing we can do with our life. You can conquer thought patters a moment at a time then for several moments a day, then daily.

Always be searching for ways to be a better you. Always be trying to improve yourself and the way you treat others.

Below there are Verses followed by Affirmation. I like to suggest to my stressed

By Robyna Smith-Keys.

Aromatherapy clients that they print out the verses and affirmation. Put them in a tin or box. Then each day shake the tin or box and pick one out. You will be amazed at how that verse and affirmation pertains to your life or day at that given time.

You will usually find that the verse you pick has a message, amazingly just for you at that moment in time. Also, surround yourself with mood lifting aromas.

Once upon a time I had a box, a pen and a notebook next to my bed. In that box, I would put notes on things I thought about. While maneuvering through my life I could never ever think of anything smart to say to someone when they slanted insults my way.

This would annoy me, to the max going to bed rehashing things I should have said. I could always think of something smart to say long after the event.

However, with age I have learned how to be at peace with others and myself. Now-days I look at people that are rude or obnoxious and smile within my heart.

They are who they are and I do not need to take on their insults nor feel anything. I do not need nor will I engage in exchanging or returning insults. I never try to defend myself when someone is telling me off. After all it is their viewpoint, they are entitled to it. However, it does stick in my mind and when the time is right I am able to set them straight in a profound way. That is the most enjoyable part of growing old, learning the art of patients and understanding and more importantly the art of response. When we are young or at least when I was young I felt the need to stand my ground and was ready in a heartbeat to take on the charging bull in anyone. Now I head for cover.

By Robyna Smith-Keys.

Mediation, Affirmation and Visualizations, have very powerful benefits. It only takes 21 days to form a habit then the habit forms you.

"Fake It Till You Make It"

Don't be a Misogynists.

Don't be a Homophobic.

Don't be a Pessimist.

Don't be anything you ought not be.

Live and Let Live

If you feel very down, pretend to everyone including yourself , that you are marvelously alive, that you feel great. Be very grateful when someone insults you. When they insult you that could mean they are either, jealous of you or fed up with you. Either way that is good to know. If they are jealous of you that means they think you have got life made.

If they are fed up with you this means, you can step out of their life without hurting them.

The other information that is most helpful when you realize that they, are fed up with you, is you have been given a warning and it is time to make some changes in your relationship. Forewarned is to be forearmed they say.

My grandfather said,

"Well girly, it's best not to say anything unless you have something very profound to say. Never return their insults with an insult. Returning an insult, is a reaction and all actions have a consequence. You are a good type of girl with a smart mind. Put pen and paper beside your bed, when you think of something smart you could have said, write it down. Then put it in a little box.

One day when you least expect it you will find you always have a verse that is a positive response to their negative actions or their hurtful words"

He went on to say,

"You cannot change the opinion of another person and they, are entitled to have an opinion. What you can change is how you feel when they give an opinion that upsets you. There is no point in being upset about their thoughts. They are they and you are you. Always mix with people that allow you to be you and you must allow them to be themselves".

"As for the other kinds of people you need to know they are probably passing through your life they are not in your life".

It is funny how something that an adult tells you when you are a wee snip of a girl can have a powerful outcome, latter on in your life.

Ba Ha Ha Happy!

The proverbs in the bible and Stephen Coveys book "Daily Reflections" have certainly helped me, at my weakest times of feeling low, confused and bewildered.

Now I have my own book and I open it every day and read at least one Verse or Affirmation. I love being in control of my emotions, and I plan to stay that way, come what may.

The hardest thing I have had to learn, is how to accept the things I have no control over. When I was young, I was an emotional cripple. Every time I heard something terrible, someone had said about me, be it true or false, I would cry my eyes out and wanted to tell them off.

Telling people off is definitely not the answer.

The greatest gift you can develop is learning how to stay silent. Leaning the difference between being a hypocrite and being genuinely

By Robyna Smith-Keys.

in control of accepting the things you cannot change.

A hypocritical person; is one who feigns some desirable or publicly approved attitude, especially one whose private life, opinions, or statements belie, contradict his or her public statements.

They are the type of person that usually gossip about others and are then extremely nice to that same persons face.

You cannot change what they have already said. It is done and dusted. You need to either learn that the person or persons listening to them will agree with them or disagree.

When they disagree, they may not say so at the time but they will not believe what the other person has said about you.

Most people are passing through your life, so why allow them to upset you. If what they have said is true then accept that, that is the way you are and laugh about it.

Tell people you know that, that is one of your shortcomings and you are working on that side of your nature.

If you laugh when you hear what has been said, other people will laugh about that side of your nature as well.

Just keep working on being a better person eventually you will get there. If what they have said is completely incorrect all you can do is calmly tell others, that it is untrue or totally incorrect. You cannot do anything about the way people see you.

You need to develop skills that most people like about you and do not enter into defending yourself unless it is vitally important. Everyone knows where the door is. If you cannot cope

By Robyna Smith-Keys.

with the people you live with or mix with you can leave.

 If they are in your home and they do not like you they can leave. If you are in a situation, where you cannot leave, then take a deep breath and release the breath slowly and smile. If you choose to stay meditate your troubles away.

Buddha said,

Buddha Was Once Asked!

What Do You Get From Meditation?

He Replied, "Nothing"!

However, Buddha Said,

Allow Me To Tell You What I Lost: Anger,
Anxiety, Depression, Insecurity, Fear Of Old
Age And Death.

By Robyna Smith-Keys.

Our life is about perfecting our experiments. As does, a scientist, who conducts his experiments with the utmost accuracy and never claims any finality about his conclusions, but keeps an open mind regarding them.

With every step we take to improve our responses to others we carry out the process of acceptance or rejection and act accordingly. Through deep self-introspection, meditation, self-talk in a positive way, we will become more in charge of our emotions and responses to others.

Nevertheless, if we refuse to experiment with a better way of controlling our tongue, mind, body and soul our life will remain unmanageable.

Most of the small to the point verses in this book are either my own inspirations gathered over time or verses I have heard or read somewhere.

Ba Ha Ha Happy!

Print them out on cardboard, place in a small box and pick one out every single day.

Remember the brain is a very powerful tool. Often our brain is confused and unable to compute. Confusion is often, caused by the use of alcohol, drugs and a lousy state of mind. All the books in the world cannot, help until you take control of those three things.

Mind: - Think good thoughts, rest and take charge of your thoughts.

Body:- Diet, exercise, posture and rest.

Soul:- Check your character and your morals are in good order. Love unconditionally.

Five sections of the brain pertain to love.

Romantic love

Self love

Sensual love

By Robyna Smith-Keys.

Parental love

Family love.

Everyones, portions will differ in size,
energized by diverse circumstances and
happenings. Exercise your mind, body and soul
in at least three ways every day.

MIND BODY SOUL
EXERCISES

Good "Body" exercises are:-

Walking fast for 20 minutes.

Turn on Music and dance around the house.

Swim

Eating five kinds' fresh fruit and vegetables.

Ba Ha Ha Happy!

Indulging in less alcohol, drugs and actions of anger.

Mediating at dawn for 5 - 10 minutes.

Drinking plenty of water.

Good "Soul" exercises are:-

Doing someone a good turn without them asking.

Never do someone a good turn unless you know for absolute certain, that is what they want.

Talk in a gentle productive way to family, friends and strangers every day.

Mediate every day.

Asking a higher power to bless your day in a positive way.

Plan to live this very day in a wonderful way.

By Robyna Smith-Keys.

Take time to listen to others effectively. No matter how short of time you are.

The most important Soul exercise of all is practice connecting to your higher power and asking for help and guidance.

I do this with a daily prayer but you can do it with a daily request.

Your Soul lives outside of you it is your protection force.

Your Soul is connected to you via your Aura field. Think of your Aura as your outer casing. A field of energy that cannot be seen most of the time but, know it is there.

Your Soul is mortal and you body is immortal.

There are components of the body, mind and soul that contribute to the flow of energy at each level. There are 'bridging mechanisms' that contribute to the overall balance and flow of energy between each level. There are things that we do in each moment that facilitate or go against our natural flow.

Read something for 10-20 minutes every day that takes mental effort to comprehend. Every day write in a diary one thing you are glad about. Then focus on all the reasons you are glad about that situation or person or thing.

Research and eat mind food.

THE LAW OF ATTRACTION

If you think about it often enough you will have it. It may differ slightly to how you saw it but you will have it. You know the old saying:-

"Be careful What You Wish for You Just Might Get It"

The Law of Attraction states that whatever you give, consistent thought too, you will create.

By Robyna Smith-Keys.

The Universe is attraction based and we get what we think about. Once you have given great thought to something with great desire and emotion, then expect it to come and it will.

Often we do attract the wrong situations and people into our life because of how we are conducting our-self. However, you must not beat yourself up about this. Every person and situation is a learning experience. The trouble I have with the "law of attraction" is- people do not attract the death of a loved one, and many other unexpected tragedies. Life has many ups and downs. Unfortunately, there is nothing, we can do to stop them. We most definitely can use the "law of attraction" to attract certain people, events and things into our life and I have proven, this to be correct many times. There are also times when we are attracted to the wrong person, thing, situation and so on. At those times of the attraction our emotions overrule our head and wham, a mistake is made. Some mistakes take decades to fix or adjust to. Therefore, we need to learn how to be happy most of the time.

ESSENTIAL OILS TO IMPROVE YOUR MIND.

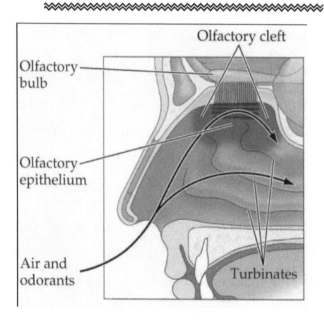

Your nose is the "factory" where odors are processed. What visual is to the eyes, olfactory is to the nose.

By Robyna Smith-Keys.

Essential oil aromas stimulate the part of the brain that affects emotion. The shape of an essential oil molecule is like a key that opens lock-like structure in the olfactory nerve receptors in our nostrils. The impression of the aroma is sent directly and immediately to the limbic system where memories are stored, pleasure and emotions are perceived.

When stimulated, the limbic system releases chemicals that affect the central nervous system. Serotonin counteracts anxiety; endorphins reduce pain and affect sexual response.

Inhaling essential oils can help us attain a pleasurable emotional balance. A balanced emotional state in turn can have a therapeutic effect on physical problems, particularly those that are stress-related.

Enhance your mental and physical well-being with essential oils using direct inhalation or diffusion. Direct inhalation is great when immediate relief is needed. For instance, to relieve stress, drip 2-5 drops of Chamomile onto a cotton -wool ball or handkerchief, hold it under your nose and breathe deeply. Because of their volatile nature, essential oils will readily diffuse into the air.

For this reason, I like to make a small bottle of sniff with a drip dropper on the top. I take the

By Robyna Smith-Keys.

lid off the bottle and sniff the oil. Then replace
the lid quickly.

ESSENTIAL OIL DIFFUSER

An aromatherapy lamp a ceramic vessel equipped with a small basin to hold a mixture of water and essential oil is a good way to diffuse scent.

The basin is warmed from underneath by a candle. Diffusing relaxing oils like Chamomile, Rose or Sandalwood can help patient's anxieties in a doctor's waiting room. The diffuser must be double glazed inside and out or it can explode.

By Robyna Smith-Keys.

To counteract after-lunch sleepiness diffuse energizing uplifting oils like Basil, Lemon, Orange, Peppermint in the office.

Note: When studying Aromatherapy we were told not to use the electric diffusers as they work against the odor molecules of the essential oils.

A bath is best taken by candle light as incandescent lights turn the odor molecules of essential oils into toxins.

Rosemary Essential Oil

Sniff the essential oil of Rosemary a few sniffs will increase your memory but do not get it on your skin.

Deep-sea fish, oysters, beetroot and green leafy vegetables are a few good brain foods. Rosemary oil has, been used by older cultures for many centuries as a mind building oil.

Ba Ha Ha Happy!

Bergamot Lifts Your Spirit.

Sniff the essential oil of Bergamot to life your mood.

Chamomile Roman For Peace

Roman Chamomile helps you to feel at peace with the way you are feeling and soothes your feelings. Such as being abandoned by the one you loved. It is also a wonderful headache relief. Rub one drop on your temples and breath slowly for a few minutes.

Cypress Helps With Transition

Cypress is calming at times of transition and when difficult changes in your life, need to be made. Cypress oil - steadies your heart after the death of a loved one.

By Robyna Smith-Keys.

Frankincense

Sniff to calm and centre yourself. A wonderful aroma when a feeling of peace is required.

Geranium Sniff for balance.

Geranium helps to even out your emotional roller-coaster.

Lavender Sniff for nurture and forgiveness

Lemon is for clarity.

Lemon helps clear your mind so that you can think clearly.

Peppermint.

Try peppermint when brainstorming. An energy booster, this scent invigorates the mind, promotes concentration and stimulates clear thinking. One drop mixed with a teaspoon of cooking oil will settle a sick stomach very quickly. Rub around the navel area. Never use of an evening as it is energizing and will prevent a restful nights sleep.

Ba Ha Ha Happy!

Rose

Sniff for compassion and Romantic love. Rose allows you to have compassion for the situation, person or yourself and to let go with love in your heart.

Note: In these pages of verses and affirmations I had a box on my dining room table filled with them. They were typed individually on cards. I would pick one each day and try to live my life in light of the verse and affirmation.   I now cannot remember all that I composed and all that are gifts from others. It was soooo very long ago. I remember I reconstructed verses too.

Either way they have helped with the design of my emotional wellbeing. I do pray they help you as well.

Plan your day and work your plan. When you conduct yourself badly,

By Robyna Smith-Keys.

Apologize.

Then try to conduct yourself better tomorrow. Whatever, you do, do not beat yourself up. The other person may have caused your misconduct but, you are only responsible for you. Keep your own counsel not the council of others.

I do not believe all that I have read in the Bible but, I have had great joy from reading it. I do not believe all the teachings of my church, my parents, my aunts and uncles. However, I have had a happy life in parts thanks to them taking the time to correct my manners, thoughts and actions. I have gained great wisdom from many parts of the Bible and the teachings of my Church. Most of all, my sanity has been gained and improved upon from studying Proverbs and Psalms, found in the Bible.

My strength, kindness towards others and my ability to look disaster in the face and deal with it, came from my mothers little tin on the dining room table. Going to church every Sunday until I was in my forties has also given me an amazing degree of faith in a power greater than myself.

AFFIRMATIONS & VERSES

Courage will only come after you have leaped into the thing you fear the most. Take that leap today.

The only thing stopping you from taking a leap of faith is **you.**

Read an affirmation or a positive spiritually uplifting verse every day and find that faith in yourself.

I feel positive that one or more of these Affirmations or Verses will help you. When you find the one that assists, lean to recite it and do so many times a day.

By Robyna Smith-Keys.

Do not wait for a tragedy to smack you in the face.

Verse

〜〜〜〜〜〜〜〜〜〜〜〜〜〜〜〜〜〜〜〜〜〜〜〜〜〜〜〜〜〜〜〜〜

*C*ourage will only come after

I have leaped into the thing

I fear the most.

Affirmation

〜〜〜〜〜〜〜〜〜〜〜〜〜〜〜〜〜〜〜〜〜〜〜〜〜〜〜〜〜〜〜〜〜

Today I will be unafraid.

Today I am powerful

Today I will be sweetly spoken yet heard.

Ba Ha Ha Happy!

〰〰〰〰〰〰〰〰〰〰〰〰〰〰〰〰〰〰〰〰〰〰

Keep you own counsel

not the counsel of others.

Affirmation

〰〰〰〰〰〰〰〰〰〰〰〰〰〰〰〰〰〰〰〰〰〰

To Day I Will Be Agreeable

I Will Mind My Own Business

I Will Only Intervene If There Is No Other
Option.

By Robyna Smith-Keys.

〰〰〰〰〰〰〰〰〰〰〰〰〰〰〰〰〰〰〰〰〰〰〰〰〰〰〰

*R*omantic Love Is Attracted By

What We Do

Not By How We Look

Do Special Things For Others

Now I See The Law Of Attraction Happen.

Affirmation

〰〰〰〰〰〰〰〰〰〰〰〰〰〰〰〰〰〰〰〰〰〰〰〰〰〰〰

I am lovable and I am becoming more
loveable every day.

I am loved and will be given expressions
of love.

True love will be mine; forever more.

Ba Ha Ha Happy!

~~~~~~

*I*f Unconditional Love Isn't Your Option

Then There Is No Commitment

Affirmation

~~~~~~

"I will accept the things I cannot change

And change the things I can".

- Abraham Lincoln

By Robyna Smith-Keys.

𝒟ress Becomingly Every Day

Come What May

Speak Softly and Passionately

Watch Your Day Blossom Your Way.

Affirmation

I will dress well every day

I will speak becomingly

I will not use slang.

Ba Ha Ha Happy!

Verse

~~~~~~

*L*ovingly At The Crack Of Dawn

Tidy Away

Then Do Something Special

For Someone Else

And Watch Love Come Your Way.

Affirmation

~~~~~~

Today I will have a plan and work my plan.

Today I will be patient, tolerant, loving and
kind.

By Robyna Smith-Keys.

Verse

~~~~~~

Love Comes In Five Ways

Goes Out In Five Ways

But Only Comes To Stay

When You Deliver Five Ways.

Affirmation

~~~~~~

I will give love in all ways, always to all I know.

I will not expect love

I will earn it.

Ba Ha Ha Happy!

〰〰〰〰〰〰〰〰〰〰〰〰〰〰〰〰〰〰〰〰〰〰〰〰〰〰

Respect You Earn

Creates Hardy Seeds

That Need Little Attention To Bloom

Affirmation

〰〰〰〰〰〰〰〰〰〰〰〰〰〰〰〰〰〰〰〰〰〰〰〰〰〰

As Of This Day

My Life Is Filled With Positive,

Happy People.

They Respect Me And Them Self.

I Will Respect All People Even If They Do Not
Respect Me Now

I Trust And Know They Will Respect Them Self
And Me Because

I Am Lovingly Patient.

By Robyna Smith-Keys.

〰〰〰〰〰〰〰〰〰〰〰〰〰〰〰〰〰〰〰〰〰

*N*o One Great Or Successful

Was Ever A Pessimist.

Be Positive

Affirmation

〰〰〰〰〰〰〰〰〰〰〰〰〰〰〰〰〰〰〰〰〰

I Will Start With A Small Thing

That I Can Be Successful At Today.

I Refuse To Be Pessimistic.

Ba Ha Ha Happy!

*D*on't Be The Victim

Stand Up For Your Rights

In A Gentle Way

Be Firm And Non- Judgmental

Affirmation

Today I Love Myself

Today I Refuse To Be Spoken To

In A Uncouth Manner.

I Will Not Respond To Ill Mannered People

I Will Feel Sorry For Them Not Me.

By Robyna Smith-Keys.

Verse

~~~~~~

*A*ll Actions Have A Consequence.

Affirmation

~~~~~~

To-day

I will pause before I speak

I will consider the end result of my words and
action.

All word bid for a response

All actions bid for a reaction.

Therefore, I will design my words and action
for a win win outcome.

Ba Ha Ha Happy!

Verse

~~~~~~

*L*ove Is Something You Do.

Love Needs A Direction

Affirmation

~~~~~~

Today I Will Show Love

Be Loving Towards Others

Expect Nothing In Return

By Robyna Smith-Keys.

Verse

~~~~~~

I Blame You For The Results

Is Not An Option I Choose.

Affirmation

~~~~~~

I Am Who I Am

You Are Who You Are

I Did What I Did

You Did What Your Did

That Is That.

I Will Never Blame Another For My Feelings.

I Will Say Sorry

I Will Accept What I Cannot Change With
Grace And Dignity.

Ba Ha Ha Happy!

~~~~~~

*F*irst Know What You Want

Go For It

Create It Begin It Now

Affirmation

~~~~~~

I Will Begin A Project To-Day

I Will Research How To Achieve

What I Want.

By Robyna Smith-Keys.

Verse

〜〜〜〜〜〜〜〜〜〜〜〜〜〜〜〜〜〜〜〜〜〜〜〜〜〜〜〜〜〜

*L*ittle Successes Lead To

Big Success. Start With

A Little One Now.

Affirmation

〜〜〜〜〜〜〜〜〜〜〜〜〜〜〜〜〜〜〜〜〜〜〜〜〜〜〜〜〜〜

To Day I Will Try What I Have Tried Before.

I Will Try And Try Again.

I Will Keep Trying On Other Days As Well.

Ba Ha Ha Happy!

~~~~~~

*H*appiness Comes From Within.

Look At Who You Are

Make Adjustments.

~~~~~~

To Day I Will Write A List

My List Will Only Contain

All The Things I Am Glad About.

By Robyna Smith-Keys.

〰〰〰〰〰〰〰〰〰〰〰〰〰〰〰〰〰〰〰〰〰〰〰〰

*L*et The Future Entice You

Out Of Your Past.

Set Your Future Plans

In Motion Today.

Affirmation

〰〰〰〰〰〰〰〰〰〰〰〰〰〰〰〰〰〰〰〰〰〰〰〰

I am Open

To Possibilities

I Will Start Carving My New Life To-Day

Ba Ha Ha Happy!

〜〜〜〜〜〜〜〜〜〜〜〜〜〜〜〜〜〜〜〜〜〜〜〜〜〜〜〜〜〜〜〜

$\mathcal{U}$se Your Own Resources

and

Create Your Own Magic

Affirmation

〜〜〜〜〜〜〜〜〜〜〜〜〜〜〜〜〜〜〜〜〜〜〜〜〜〜〜〜〜〜〜〜

Magic Happens

Today I Am Ready

For Magic To Happen.

I Have Many Talents

I Have Many Gifts

By Robyna Smith-Keys.

Let Go Of The Past

It Has No Bearing On Tomorrow

Start Living Now.

Affirmation

Today I Ask My Higher Power For
_____(name what you want)

I Trust I Will Have It In Due Course.

Ba Ha Ha Happy!

~~~~~~

*D*reams Do Come True.

Dream It.

Do It.

I am Living the Life I Have Created.

~~~~~~

To Day I Will Take A Deep Breath.

I Will Focus On An Impossible Dream.

Because I Do Believe

Dreams Do Come True.

By Robyna Smith-Keys.

Verse

~~~~~~

*D*on't Take Your Cares

Into The Next Second.

Push Them Out Of

Your Mind Now.

Affirmation

~~~~~~

Today Every Time I Think Of Negative Things.

I Will Say.

If I Cannot Fix It Now.

I Will Not Think about It Now.

Ba Ha Ha Happy!

*A*t Any Given Moment

You Can Start A New.

Simply Make Up

Your Mind And Do It.

Affirmation

Today I Will Change Just One Moment In My
Life

Tomorrow I Will Change Two Moments In My
Life

I Will Keep Changing Moments Until

They Become Life Changing Events

That I Am Proud Of.

By Robyna Smith-Keys.

Verse

~~~~~~

*L*earn To Walk Before You Run

One Step At A Time.

Even If It Takes A Lifetime

You'll Make It.

Verse

~~~~~~

The Largest Mountain

Can Be Climbed With

The Right Tools.

Search For Them Now.

Ba Ha Ha Happy!

*T*here Is Magic

In Listening. So Talk Less

And Listen More.

Today I Will Listen Intently

I Will Not Interrupt Others

Today Is About Listening To Others.

Even If I Disagree I Will Not Say So

By Robyna Smith-Keys.

~~~~~~

When It Is Raining

There Is Plenty I Can Do

I Am Thankful For The Rain.

Affirmation

~~~~~~

To Day I Will Plan My Day

Around The Weather

I Will Accomplish Great Things.

Ba Ha Ha Happy!

〰〰〰〰〰〰〰〰〰〰〰〰〰〰〰〰〰〰〰〰〰〰〰〰〰

*U*nconditional Love

Builds Hope & Great Joy.

〰〰〰〰〰〰〰〰〰〰〰〰〰〰〰〰〰〰〰〰〰〰〰〰〰

Today I Will Not Try To Change

The Ones I Love

I Will Show Them I Love Them
Unconditionally

I Will Tell Them I Love Them

Unconditionally.

By Robyna Smith-Keys.

〜〜〜〜〜〜〜〜〜〜〜〜〜〜〜〜〜〜〜〜〜〜〜〜〜〜〜〜〜〜〜〜〜〜〜

*I*t All Begins With Me.

.

Affirmation

〜〜〜〜〜〜〜〜〜〜〜〜〜〜〜〜〜〜〜〜〜〜〜〜〜〜〜〜〜〜〜〜〜〜〜

Today I Will Be Different

I Will Be Charming And Funny

To All Those I Know.

I will accept who they are and still be

who I have designed.

Ba Ha Ha Happy!

∿∿∿∿∿∿∿∿∿∿∿∿∿∿∿∿∿∿∿∿∿∿∿∿∿∿∿∿∿

*S*trengthen Friendships With

Kind Words And Deeds.

Never Point Out Any Ones Faults.

Affirmation

∿∿∿∿∿∿∿∿∿∿∿∿∿∿∿∿∿∿∿∿∿∿∿∿∿∿∿∿∿

Every Time I Am About To Say Something

I Will Think First

Of The Response I Will Get

Before I Utter A Single Word.

∿∿∿∿∿∿∿∿∿∿∿∿∿∿∿∿∿∿∿∿∿∿∿∿∿∿∿∿∿

By Robyna Smith-Keys.

〜〜〜〜〜〜〜〜〜〜〜〜〜〜〜〜〜〜〜〜〜〜〜〜〜〜〜〜〜

*Y*ou Cannot Climb The Ladder Of Success

Dressed In The Costume Of Failure.

- Zig Ziglar

Affirmation

〜〜〜〜〜〜〜〜〜〜〜〜〜〜〜〜〜〜〜〜〜〜〜〜〜〜〜〜〜

To Day I Will Dress In My Best

Today I Will Look Becomingly

Even When I Am At Home I Will Be Clean And
Tidy.

My Good Look Will Inspire Others

Ba Ha Ha Happy!

〜〜〜〜〜〜〜〜〜〜〜〜〜〜〜〜〜〜〜〜〜〜〜〜〜〜〜〜〜〜〜〜〜〜〜〜

*S*et A Plan

In Motion Right Now.

Have A Strategy, A Program.

Affirmation
〜〜〜〜〜〜〜〜〜〜〜〜〜〜〜〜〜〜〜〜〜〜〜〜〜〜〜〜〜〜〜〜〜〜〜〜

To Day

I Will Write Down The Six Most Important
Things To Do.

I Will Work Through This Plan

I will live my life by design

By Robyna Smith-Keys.

~~~~~~

*T*he Puzzles Of Personalities

Are Accumulations Of

Circumstances and Happenings.

Affirmation
~~~~~~

Today I Will Not Try To Unravel The Puzzle

Of Peoples Personalities

I Will Accept Who They Are

And Enjoy Their Quirks.

Ba Ha Ha Happy!

~~~~~~

*F*ailure & Grief Come

From Indecision.

Act Now Rectify Later

If The Need Arises.

Affirmation

~~~~~~

Today I Will Be Happy As My Grief Moves
Slowly Out Of My Life.

Today I Will Rectify What I Can

Accept What I Cannot

Rectify Right Now.

By Robyna Smith-Keys.

〰〰〰〰〰〰〰〰〰〰〰〰〰〰〰〰〰〰〰〰〰〰

*I*t is the mark of an educated mind to be able

to entertain a thought without accepting it.

-Aristotle

Affirmation

〰〰〰〰〰〰〰〰〰〰〰〰〰〰〰〰〰〰〰〰〰〰

When a thought comes to mind I will asses it.

I will be calm and think of the thought with
three outcomes.

Verse

~~~~~~

*L*ying for personal gain, seeks to ensnare,

enslave, entrap and destroy you and others.

Be you that lies.
Your way to a full life is burdened.

Your life will be purer saner more fulfilling
when you step out of the liars web.

Affirmation For Liar

~~~~~~

My Practice to deceive will end this day
I am truly sorry for my way
I will be truthful come what may.

Affirmation for the entrapped.

~~~~~~

I no long fall for your liars

I will take back my power

I will be happy

By Robyna Smith-Keys.

VERSES

Verse

" *I* have learned the value of old friends by

making many new ones."

– Abraham Lincoln

Verse

*K*eep The End In Mind

But Begin Now.

With A Kind And Open Heart.

Verse

〜〜〜〜〜〜〜〜〜〜〜〜〜〜〜〜〜〜〜〜〜〜〜〜〜

"**A**lways bear in mind that your own resolution to succeed, is more important than any other one thing."

– Abraham Lincoln

Verse

〜〜〜〜〜〜〜〜〜〜〜〜〜〜〜〜〜〜〜〜〜〜〜〜〜

"**W**e can complain because rose bushes have thorns."

-Abraham Lincoln

With this verse by Abraham Lincoln know that sometimes it is right to complain. An evil force (the devil) only needs one good person to stay silent for him-(the evil force), to create what seems like an attractive idea that turns into chaos / pandemonium.

By Robyna Smith-Keys.

〜〜〜〜〜〜〜〜〜〜〜〜〜〜〜〜〜〜〜〜〜〜〜〜〜〜〜〜〜〜〜

*M*editate For Five Minutes

Every Day About The Person

You Would Like To Be.

〜〜〜〜〜〜〜〜〜〜〜〜〜〜〜〜〜〜〜〜〜〜〜〜〜〜〜〜〜〜〜

*Y*ou Have A Higher Power

Tap Into It By Talking

To Yourself About Your Needs,

You Dreams

Ba Ha Ha Happy!

Verse

〰〰〰〰〰〰〰〰〰〰〰〰〰〰〰〰〰〰〰〰〰〰〰〰

*Y*ou May Think You Are A

Kind Soul

But What Do Others

Think Of You.

Verse

〰〰〰〰〰〰〰〰〰〰〰〰〰〰〰〰〰〰〰〰〰〰〰〰

*D*on't Think

Act Now

With Passion

By Robyna Smith-Keys.

~~~~~~

*T*o Be Loved Unconditionally

Love Another More Than

All The Grains Of Sand Upon

All The Beaches.

Verse

~~~~~~

*D*o Someone A Good Turn

And Keep It To Yourself.

If Anyone Finds Out It Will Not Count.

Ba Ha Ha Happy!

〜〜〜〜〜〜〜〜〜〜〜〜〜〜〜〜〜〜〜〜〜〜〜〜〜〜〜〜〜〜〜〜〜〜

Keep You Own Council

Leave It To A Higher Power

To Unravel The Mind Puzzles Of Others.

Verse

〜〜〜〜〜〜〜〜〜〜〜〜〜〜〜〜〜〜〜〜〜〜〜〜〜〜〜〜〜〜〜〜〜〜

The More We Do The More

We Accomplish. Don't Waste Time

O r Time Will Waste You

Your Mind & Your Body

By Robyna Smith-Keys.

〰〰〰〰〰〰〰〰〰〰〰〰〰〰〰〰〰〰〰〰〰〰〰〰〰〰

" *I*ntellect Is Not A God

It Has Of Course The Power To

Create Miracles

But Without Personality."

~By Albert Einstein.

Verse

〰〰〰〰〰〰〰〰〰〰〰〰〰〰〰〰〰〰〰〰〰〰〰〰〰〰

" *W*hoever undertakes to set himself up as

judge in the field of truth and knowledge is
shipwrecked by the laughter of the Gods."

~By Albert Einstein.

Verse

〜〜〜〜〜〜〜〜〜〜〜〜〜〜〜〜〜〜〜〜〜〜〜〜〜〜〜

" *G*reat spirits have always found violent

opposition from mediocre minds. The latter
cannot understand it when a man does not
thoughtlessly submit to hereditary prejudices
but honestly and courageously uses his
intelligence."

~By Albert Einstein.

Verse

〜〜〜〜〜〜〜〜〜〜〜〜〜〜〜〜〜〜〜〜〜〜〜〜〜〜〜〜〜〜〜

" *W*hoever undertakes to set himself up as

judge in the field of truth and knowledge is
shipwrecked by the laughter of the Gods."

~By Albert Einstein.

By Robyna Smith-Keys.

〰〰〰〰〰〰〰〰〰〰〰〰〰〰〰〰〰〰〰〰〰〰〰〰〰

"*T*he ideals which have lighted me on my way

and time after time given me new courage to face life cheerfully, have been Truth, Goodness, and Beauty".

~Albert Einstein.

Verse

〰〰〰〰〰〰〰〰〰〰〰〰〰〰〰〰〰〰〰〰〰〰〰〰〰

*C*apitalize On What You Can Do.

The Greatest Of Men Have Not

Been Great Scholars.

Ba Ha Ha Happy!

~~~~~~

A Win Is Really A Loss

When A Win Harms Another.

~~~~~~

*D*eceit Seems Sweet But

Will Only End

In Defeat

By Robyna Smith-Keys.

~~~~~~

*W*e Are Nothing

Without The Input Of Others.

Be They Of Grand

Or Simple Of Mind.

Verse

~~~~~~

*D*on't Fear The Gossip's Tongue

Their Sour Thoughts Shall Disease

Their Bones.

Two Wrongs Don't Make A Right.

Ba Ha Ha Happy!

~~~~~~

*R*esist Fear With All Your Might

And Courage Will Endow You

With Wealth

~~~~~~

*S*uffering Has A Unique Reward

Called Experience Known As

The Greatest Gift To Man.

By Robyna Smith-Keys.

〜〜〜〜〜〜〜〜〜〜〜〜〜〜〜〜〜〜〜〜〜〜〜〜〜〜〜

*K*nowledge Is In Our Heart.

Wisdom In Our Soul.

Judgment Is

Unwise-Wisdom.

Verse

〜〜〜〜〜〜〜〜〜〜〜〜〜〜〜〜〜〜〜〜〜〜〜〜〜〜〜

*L*ife Is A Mystery To Be Lived.

Not A Problem

To Be Solved.

Ba Ha Ha Happy!

Verse

〰〰〰〰〰〰〰〰〰〰〰〰〰〰〰〰〰〰〰〰

*L*augh Your Head Off Right Now.

Cry To No One And

Gather Friends.

Verse

〰〰〰〰〰〰〰〰〰〰〰〰〰〰〰〰〰〰〰〰

*C*ourage Is Never Tested

Until The Day Of Your Death.

Be Afraid Of Nothing Less.

By Robyna Smith-Keys.

Verse

〰〰〰〰〰〰〰〰〰〰〰〰〰〰〰〰〰〰〰〰〰〰

A Real Wish Is To Love,

Be Loved And Tempted By

Nothing Nor Anyone

Verse

〰〰〰〰〰〰〰〰〰〰〰〰〰〰〰〰〰〰〰〰〰〰

*B*efore Advising Anyone

Ask Yourself

Have I Ever Been

In His Shoes

With His Life's Conditions

Ba Ha Ha Happy!

〜〜〜〜〜〜〜〜〜〜〜〜〜〜〜〜〜〜〜〜〜〜〜〜〜〜〜

*P*aradise Is A Superficial Place

Unless Your Humble.

〜〜〜〜〜〜〜〜〜〜〜〜〜〜〜〜〜〜〜〜〜〜〜〜〜〜〜

*I*n A Husbands Absence No Man

Should Cross Your

Door Step

By Robyna Smith-Keys.

Verse

Verse

~~~~~~

For Real Relief Reveal Everything

There Is To Know

Let The Chips Fall Where They May.

Verse

~~~~~~

No Longer Be Addicted

To The Pleasure

Of Your Senses

Ba Ha Ha Happy!

〰〰〰〰〰〰〰〰〰〰〰〰〰〰〰〰〰〰〰〰〰〰〰

*T*here is A Law Of Return

Be Patient And Have Faith

Good Times Return

〰〰〰〰〰〰〰〰〰〰〰〰〰〰〰〰〰〰〰〰〰〰〰

*R*e-Connect To Silence Within You.

Instead Of Waiting For Life Or Others

To Calm Down,

Choose To Be Calm.

By Robyna Smith-Keys.

Verse

Verse

〰〰〰〰〰〰〰〰〰〰〰〰〰〰〰〰〰〰〰〰〰〰〰

Keep Trying To Be Happy

Believe In Great Things

Then A Great Life To You

Will Be Granted.

Verse

〰〰〰〰〰〰〰〰〰〰〰〰〰〰〰〰〰〰〰〰〰〰〰

Don't Take Your Cares

Into The Next Second.

Push Them Out Of

Your Mind Now.

Ba Ha Ha Happy!

〰〰〰〰〰〰〰〰〰〰〰〰〰〰〰〰〰〰〰〰〰〰〰〰

*A*t Any Given Moment You Can

Start A New

Simply Make Up

Your Mind And Do It.

.

〰〰〰〰〰〰〰〰〰〰〰〰〰〰〰〰〰〰〰〰〰〰〰〰

*I*n Every Living Person Or Thing

There Is Goodness

All You Have To Do Is

Look For It.

By Robyna Smith-Keys.

Verse

~~~~~~

*A*n Idea Is Nothing

Without Action

Surge On

With All The Force You Can Muster.

Verse

~~~~~~

*Y*ou Cannot Climb To Success

By Pushing Others Down.

Take Each Step Carefully.

Ba Ha Ha Happy!

〜〜〜〜〜〜〜〜〜〜〜〜〜〜〜〜〜〜〜〜〜〜〜〜〜〜

*T*urn On Your Personal Magnetism

And Charm

And See What Magic

It Can Do For You.

〜〜〜〜〜〜〜〜〜〜〜〜〜〜〜〜〜〜〜〜〜〜〜〜〜〜

*U*se The Warmth Of Your Voice

To Convey The Warmth

Of Your Heart.

By Robyna Smith-Keys.

Verse

~~~~~~

Optimism Is A Matter Of

Mental Habit Forced Thinking

In The Affirmative Soon

Becomes Natural.

Verse

~~~~~~

Keep You Own Council

Leave It To

A Higher Power To Unravel

The Puzzles Of Others.

.

Ba Ha Ha Happy!

〜〜〜〜〜〜〜〜〜〜〜〜〜〜〜〜〜〜〜〜〜〜〜〜〜〜〜〜〜

*F*ailure And Grief

Come From Indecision.

Act Now Rectify Later

If The Need Arises.

〜〜〜〜〜〜〜〜〜〜〜〜〜〜〜〜〜〜〜〜〜〜〜〜〜〜〜〜〜

*W*inning And Losing

Are Both Habits.

If You are Losing

Change Your Habits.

By Robyna Smith-Keys.

Verse

~~~~~~

*M*ore People Rust Out

Rather Than Wear Out.

So Work And Study

For At Least

Twelve Hours Per Day.

.

Verse

~~~~~~

*T*o Be A Good Wife

You Have To Be

A Good Actress

Ba Ha Ha Happy!

Verse

~~~~~~

*W*hen We Practice To Deceive

Oh What A Low Life We Weave

Which Tangles Us Beyond Believe.

Verse

~~~~~~

*T*he Fear Of The LORD Is

The Beginning Of Knowledge,

Only Fools Despise

Wisdom And Instruction.

- The Holy Bible.

By Robyna Smith-Keys.

〰〰〰〰〰〰〰〰〰〰〰〰〰〰〰〰〰〰〰〰〰〰〰〰〰〰〰〰

*M*agic Sometimes Means Tricks.

Magick Always Means

It Will Happen

If You Believe It Will.

Believe In Great Things

Furthermore A Great Life

To You

Will Be Granted.

Verse

〰〰〰〰〰〰〰〰〰〰〰〰〰〰〰〰〰〰〰〰〰〰〰

Enjoy and Energize

This Day

This Very Moment

Yesterday Is Gone.

Tomorrow Is Unborn.

All We Have Is Right Now

So Live It

Enjoy It

Energize It.

By Robyna Smith-Keys.

〜〜〜〜〜〜〜〜〜〜〜〜〜〜〜〜〜〜〜〜〜〜〜〜〜〜〜〜

" *O*h, What A Tangled Web

We Weave...When First

We Practice To Deceive."

— Walter Scott, Marmion

〜〜〜〜〜〜〜〜〜〜〜〜〜〜〜〜〜〜〜〜〜〜〜〜〜〜〜〜

*W*hen We Practice To Deceive

We Weave A Web

That Others See

Which Tangles Us Beyond Believe.

Ba Ha Ha Happy!

Verse

~~~~~~

*T*ic, Tic, Tock Goes The Clock

Every Second Counts

Busy I Will Be

Do It Now...... No Need!

Plants A Dangerous Seed

Verse

~~~~~~

*S*ome Say It Is Better

Late Than Never

But Once The Boat Is Gone

It Is Gone.

By Robyna Smith-Keys.

〰〰〰〰〰〰〰〰〰〰〰〰〰〰〰〰〰〰〰〰〰〰〰〰〰

Burn Your Desires

With Intense Strength

For Only Then Will Nothing

Be Beyond Your Reach.

Verse

〰〰〰〰〰〰〰〰〰〰〰〰〰〰〰〰〰〰〰〰〰〰〰〰〰

In Every Living Person

Or Thing

There Is Goodness

All You Have To Do Is Look For It.

Ba Ha Ha Happy!

An Idea Is Nothing

Without Action.

Surge On

With All The Force You Can Muster.

A life without obedience to our higher

power is a life of bad design.

By Robyna Smith-Keys.

Verse

$\mathcal{Y}$ou Cannot Climb To Success

By Pushing Others Down.

Take Each Step Carefully.

Verse

$\mathcal{T}$urn On Your Personal Magnetism

And Charm

And See What Magic

It Can Do For You.

Verse

~~~~~~

*U*se The Warmth Of Your Voice

To Convey The Warmth

Of Your Heart.

Verse

~~~~~~

*O*ptimism Is A Matter Of

Mental Habit.

Forced Thinking

In The Affirmative Soon

Becomes Natural.

By Robyna Smith-Keys.

〜〜〜〜〜〜〜〜〜〜〜〜〜〜〜〜〜〜〜〜〜〜〜〜〜〜〜〜〜〜

*S*often Your Expression

And Your Thoughts

It Will Soften Others

Towards you.

Verse

〜〜〜〜〜〜〜〜〜〜〜〜〜〜〜〜〜〜〜〜〜〜〜〜〜〜〜〜〜〜

*P*lant Seeds Of Positive Thoughts

Watch Them Grow.

To Plant Nothing

Is Directionless

Ba Ha Ha Happy!

~~~~~~

*S*uccess Is Nothing

Unless You Are A Person Of

Graciousness And Decency.

~~~~~~

*N*ever Worry About

What Might Happen.

Concentrate

On What

You'd Like To Happen.

By Robyna Smith-Keys.

Verse

〜〜〜〜〜〜〜〜〜〜〜〜〜〜〜〜〜〜〜〜〜〜〜〜〜〜〜〜〜〜

*B*efore Someone Asks

Lend A Hand This Will Strengthen

Your Heart and Eradicate Your Fears.

Verse

〜〜〜〜〜〜〜〜〜〜〜〜〜〜〜〜〜〜〜〜〜〜〜〜〜〜〜〜〜〜

*G*ather Friends That Inspire

Encourage

And.

Nourish You

No Plant Improves

Without Water.

138

Ba Ha Ha Happy!

〰〰〰〰〰〰〰〰〰〰〰〰〰〰〰〰〰〰〰〰〰〰〰

*F*or The Want Of Instruction

A Child Is Lost.

Verse

〰〰〰〰〰〰〰〰〰〰〰〰〰〰〰〰〰〰〰〰〰〰〰

*M*alevolence Is In Us All

As Is Integrity

Most Of Mankind Choose Integrity

In Assortment Of Degrees

By Robyna Smith-Keys.

〜〜〜〜〜〜〜〜〜〜〜〜〜〜〜〜〜〜〜〜〜〜〜〜〜〜〜〜〜〜〜〜

You Are The Ruler

Of Your Fate

The Guardian Of Your Soul

The Keeper Of

Your Mind.

The Guard of Your Character.

Plan Your Fate By Searching

For Best Behavior Lifestyle.

〜〜〜〜〜〜〜〜〜〜〜〜〜〜〜〜〜〜〜〜〜〜〜〜〜〜〜〜〜〜〜〜

Ba Ha Ha Happy!

~~~~~~

*M*agic Moments Can Be Yours

Look At The Stars Make A Wish

And Take Their Dazzle Into Your Life.

Verse

~~~~~~

*B*efore Someone Asks

Lend A Hand
This Will Strengthen
Your Heart &
Eradicate Your Fears.

By Robyna Smith-Keys.

Verse

〜〜〜〜〜〜〜〜〜〜〜〜〜〜〜〜〜〜〜〜〜〜〜〜〜〜〜〜〜〜

*G*ather Friends That Inspire You

And Encourage You.

No Plant Is Nourished

Without Water.

Verse

〜〜〜〜〜〜〜〜〜〜〜〜〜〜〜〜〜〜〜〜〜〜〜〜〜〜〜〜〜〜

*Y*ou Are The Ruler

Of Your Fate The Guardian

Of Your Soul And The Keeper Of

Your Mind.

Ba Ha Ha Happy!

〜〜〜〜〜〜〜〜〜〜〜〜〜〜〜〜〜〜〜〜〜〜〜〜〜〜〜〜〜〜〜〜

*T*o Keep Your Authentic Values

In Tact

Is Your Responsibility.

Be Dependable.

Verse

〜〜〜〜〜〜〜〜〜〜〜〜〜〜〜〜〜〜〜〜〜〜〜〜〜〜〜〜〜〜〜〜

*R*eady to fight be a fool

Not Ready At All more foolish he be

Ready to agree to disagree

The smart folk be

By Robyna Smith-Keys.

〰〰〰〰〰〰〰〰〰〰〰〰〰〰〰〰〰〰〰〰〰〰〰〰〰

"*D*rugs Lift My Mood

Then Desecrate My Life"   .

〰〰〰〰〰〰〰〰〰〰〰〰〰〰〰〰〰〰〰〰〰〰〰〰〰

*L*ife has no worth without people be
they good or bad.

.

Ba Ha Ha Happy!

Verse

~~~~~~

$\mathcal{D}$esign and structure your life or crumbs

without decent friends will be your eternal life.

~~~~~~
LAUGH VERSE
~~~~~~

$\mathcal{L}$aughter Is All That I Need

It Is Food For My Soul Indeed

I Will Never Ever Use Weed

Alcohol I Not Need

True Laughter Is A Pure Deed,

Indeed.

Ba Ha Ha Ha Ha

By Robyna Smith-Keys.

*T*o-Day I Will Laugh Out Loud.

I Will Find Three Things

To Make Me Laugh.

I Will Laugh

I Will Get Over Myself And Laugh

Even If It Is At My Own Stupidity

I Will Laugh.

Ba Ha Ha Happy!

*T*here Are Three Types Of Sin

Venial

Mortal

And Cardinal Sins

Affirmation
~~~~~~

I Pray To Never Ever Be Faced With

The Temptation To Commit

Mortal And Cardinal Sins.

I Will Admit To My Higher Power I Have
Sinned And Accept My Forgiveness

By Robyna Smith-Keys.

Our spoken words are Affirmations. Therefore, if we speak out loud it will come our way. Be-careful in your life to only speak in a positive way.

"We cannot solve a problem with the same mentality that created it."

~ Albert Einstein ~

Making lists is very important. Each list is considered a goal. One goal list is all the things that cause you to stay in a difficult state.

The other list is how to work at getting out of that state. The next list is the things you are going to have. Put times next to the things you are going to have.

Send love to your fears. I mean literally say out loud I send love to _____. List all of the things that you feel are holding you back from accomplishing your goals.

Then list all the things that you plan to commit too in order to achieve your goals. If you have a note pad on your phone write down your weekly plan on how to change things. Have a savings plan. Go without something so you can save. Talk yourself out of things you do not need and put that money aside.

An Anxiety-disorder is when you fear something and become anxious about it. You may or may not know what you fear.

Anxiety is often, triggered by stress and stress is triggered by fear of something, someone or the unknown answer to a situation. Some people are more vulnerable to anxiety than others, but even those who become anxious easily can learn to manage it well.

By Robyna Smith-Keys.

There is a law of attraction. Your thoughts are powerful magnets and you will get what you consistently think about whether you want it or not.

Most angry people have a need to be in the right. They are easily annoyed, irritated, aggravated or goaded.

It is important to understand that everyone has their own set of standards. It is impossible for everyone to see or feel the way you do.

To "agree to disagree" is a priceless frame of mind. Everyone has mountains of thoughts and moral codes by which they live. You cannot move a mountain without either dynamite or thousands of strong men and thousands of hours. You do not need to agree with anyone but you do need to develop the art of:

"Agreeing To Disagree"

Ba Ha Ha Happy!

This means that you understand that neither of you, are going to agree and you have both agreed that you see and feel things differently.

If your partner, friends and family, do not challenge you, you will remain ordinary.

Your attitude, approach, manner, should be your altitude. Not your damnation.

By Robyna Smith-Keys.

AFFIRMATIONS FOR
ANXIETY

Think These Words As You Are Breathing Slowly In And Out.

I Am Cool,

I Am Calm And Collected.

As I Breath In I Feel Calm

As I Exhale I Push Tension Away

As I Breath In Every Cell In My Body

Is Relaxed And Oozes With Calmness.

While Holding Your Breathe In Say Calm, Calm I Am Calm

As I Breathe Out

I Love Myself Deeply And Unconditionally.

AFFIRMATIONS FOR ANGER

Anger is the mission reaction to being insulted. It must be controlled.

As I am slowly and deeply breathing in and slowly out-I focus on the things that make me angry.

I release these feelings as I am slowly breathing in and out.

I will not be angry.

I feel calm, I am slowly breathing in and slowly breathing out. I feel gentle and calm. Very calm.

I will be understanding.

I will feel love toward those that anger me.

I will act differently towards those that anger me.

By Robyna Smith-Keys.

I will show unconditional love.

They are not in this world to live up to my expectations.

I am not in this world to live up to their expectations.

I will be myself and allow them to be their self.

As I breathe deeply in and slowly out, I will focus on what I can change.

I will understand what I cannot change.

I will accept these things and be calm.

Today I am truthful, brave and cool tempered.

Ba Ha Ha Happy!

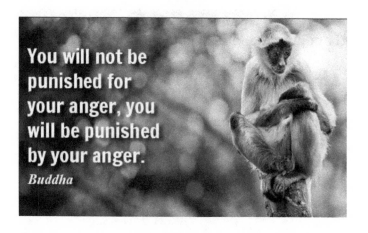

You Will Not Be

Punished By Anger,

You Will Be Punished

By Your Anger.

- Buddha

By Robyna Smith-Keys.

PROSPERITY AFFIRMATION

I am jumping into an abundant life.

I am living in a beautiful home.

I have many wonderful friends.

I have family that love me.

I have money in the bank for rainy days.

All my bills get paid on time

I have transport to all venues I need to attend.

I am happy because I have made up my mind to be that way.

No one can hurt me because- I like, who I am and the person I am becoming.

~~~ *** ~~~

Anything you want, say you have it and be thankful for it. You may think it is impossible to have these things but if you truly believe, you have them and keep believing it eventually you will have them. Miracles do happen.

A young woman that worked for me-as a massage therapist has a child that was born with difficulties. She was told, he would never lead a normal life and he would never walk.

Every morning she would massage him and say,

"You have a lovely strong body and lovely strong legs".

As a small boy, he wore braces to help his legs stay straight. Other children would call him names, he would come back at them with that tried and true verse.

"Sticks and stones will break my bones but names will never hurt me".

By Robyna Smith-Keys.

Then they would come back at him with things like but your bones are rotten you cannot walk without irons to support you.

"Yes! I am very lucky and my family has taught me to be kind to others".

His mother would prepare him to come back at the bullies and work on building his confidence.

Now he is a normal teenager and walks just like other teenagers. She never gave up and still chants for each of her children every day.

With my friends story in mind-learn to be positive; learn to like yourself by doing what is right at all costs. Prepare your children to cope with bullies teach them verses and it will help them to be able to say something smart and non-reactive.

~~~~~~
VERSES BY OTHERS
~~~~~~

"*L*ife is a great big canvas,

you should throw all the paint on it

you can."

- Francisca

"*L*ive life fully while you're here.

Experience everything. Take care of yourself and your friends. Have fun; be crazy; be weird. Go out and screw up! You're going to anyway, so you might as well enjoy the process."

- Anthony Robbins

By Robyna Smith-Keys.

"*S*o much sadness exists in the world

that we are all under obligation to contribute as much joy as lies within our powers."

- John Sutherland Bonnell

"*W*e always have enough to be happy

if we are enjoying what we do have - and not worrying about what we don't have."

- Ken Keyes, Jr.

"*L*ife is too short to worry about stupid

things. Have fun. Fall in love. Regret nothing, and don't let people bring you down."

- Unknown Author

"*M*oney in itself won't make you

happy. But money can buy you the freedom to do the things that can make you happy. True happiness comes from filling your time and your days with meaningful pursuits that you're passionate about."

- Unknown Author

"*H*appiness depends on what you can

give, not on what you can get."

- Swami Chinmayananda

By Robyna Smith-Keys.

"*T*rue happiness cannot be found in

things that change and pass away.
Pleasure and pain alternate inexorably.
Happiness comes from the self and can
be found in the self only. Find your real
self and all else will come with it."

- Nisargadatta Maharaj

"*Y*ou can't have a better tomorrow if

you are thinking about yesterday all the
time."

- Charles Fran

"*I*t is not length of life,

but depth of life."

- Ralph Waldo Emerson

" *The* purpose of life is the expansion

of happiness."

– Maharishi Mahesh Yogi

" *Many* people chase after success.

Others pursue money. But I think the happiest people on earth are the one's who have found significance. The real question of life must be – what has significance for you?"

– Unknown Author

" *He* that is of a merry heart hasth a

continual feast."

– Biblical Proverb

By Robyna Smith-Keys.

"*W*hen you learn to accept instead of
expect, you'll have fewer
disappointments."

- Robert Fisher

"*W*orrying does not take away
tomorrow's troubles. It takes away
today's peace."

- Randy Armstrong

"*P*eople have a hard time letting go of
their suffering. Out of a fear of the
unknown, they prefer suffering
that is familiar."

- Thich Nhat Hanh

164

"*H*appiness is like a sunbeam, which

the least shadow intercepts, while
adversity is often as the rain of spring."

- Chinese Proverb

"*H*appiness cannot be traveled to,

owned, earned, worn or consumed.
Happiness is the spiritual experience of
living every minute with love, grace, and
gratitude."

- Denis Waitley

"*G*arner up pleasant thoughts in your
mind, for pleasant thoughts make
pleasant lives."

- John Wilkins

By Robyna Smith-Keys.

" *B*etter by far you should forget and smile

than that you should remember and be sad."

- Christina Georgina Rossetti

" *A*nd could you keep your heart in wonder at

the daily miracles of your life, your pain would
not seem less wondrous than your joy."

- Kahlil Gibran

" *L*ook in the mirror every day and say,

I am in charge. You might not have
control over every phase of your life, but
you have more control than you realize,
and you are responsible for your own
happiness and success."

- Harvey Mackay

166

" *G*ratitude unlocks the fullness of life.

It turns what we have into enough, and more. It turns denial into acceptance, chaos to order, confusion to clarity. It can turn a meal into a feast, a house into a home, a stranger into a friend. Gratitude makes sense of our past, brings peace for today, and creates a vision for tomorrow."

- Melody Beattie

" *R*ealize deeply that the present

moment is all you ever have."

- Eckhart Tolle

By Robyna Smith-Keys.

"*L*ife's greatest happiness is to be

convinced we are loved."

- Victor Hugo

"*W*hen you get to the end of your

rope, tie a knot and hang on."

- Franklin Delano Roosevelt

"*A*fter all it is those who have a deep

and real inner life who are best able to
deal with the irritating details of outer
life."

- Evelyn Underhill

"*T*he secret of joy in work is contained in one word - excellence. To know how to do something well is to enjoy it."

- Pearl Buck

"*N*o matter how far you fall into negativity, there is always a way out."

- Karen Berg

"*E*njoy your own life without comparing it with that of another."

- Marquis de Condorcet

By Robyna Smith-Keys.

"*B*e in love with your life.

Every minute of it."

- Jack Kerouac

"*T*he [person] who reads nothing at all
is better educated than the [person] who
reads nothing but newspapers."

- Thomas Jefferson

"*W*hen you relinquish the desire to
control your future, you can have more
happiness."

- Nicole Kidman

"*The* indispensable first step to getting

the things you want out of life is this, decide what you want."

- Ben Stein

"*The* positive thinker sees the invisible,

feels the intangible, and achieves the impossible."

- Anonymous

"*Write* the bad things that are done to

you in sand, but write the good things that happen to you on a piece of marble."

- Arabic Parable

By Robyna Smith-Keys.

"*A*re you bored with life? Then throw

yourself into some work you believe in
with all your heart, live for it, die for it,
and you will find happiness that you had
thought could never be yours."

- Dale Carnegie

"*L*ife is not measured by the breaths

we take, but by the moments that take
our breath away."

- Unknown Author

"*W*e learn the inner secret of

happiness when we learn to direct our
inner drives, our interest and our
attention to something outside
ourselves."

- Ethel Perry Andrus

"*H*ope smiles from the threshold of the year to come, whispering, 'It will be happier.'"

- Alfred Lord Tennyson

"*I*t is how we feel about ourselves that provides the greatest reward from any activity. It is not what we get that makes us valuable, it is what we become in the process of doing that brings value into our lives."

- Jim Rohn

"*Y*our living is determined not so much by what life brings to you as by the attitude you bring to life; not so much by what happens to you as by the way your mind looks at what happens."

- Khalil Gibran

By Robyna Smith-Keys.

"*G*et happiness out of your work or you

may never know what happiness is."

- Elbert Hubbard

"*H*appiness is not achieved by the

conscious pursuit of happiness; it is
generally the by-product of other
activities."

- Aldous Huxley

"*M*ay your walls know joy, may every

room hold laughter and every window
open to great possibility."

- Maryanne Radmacher-Hershey

"*It* isn't what you have or who you are

or where you are or what you are doing that makes you happy or unhappy. It is what you think about it."

- Dale Carnegie

"*That* is happiness: To be dissolved into something complete and great."

- Willa Cather

"*He* who is not contented with what he

has, would not be contented with what he would like to have."

- Socrates

By Robyna Smith-Keys.

"*H*appiness comes from within. It is

not dependent on external things or on
other people. You become vulnerable
and can be easily hurt when your
feelings of security and happiness
depend on the behavior and actions of
other people. Never give your power to
anyone else."

- Brian L. Weiss

"*N*ever be afraid to sit awhile and

think."

- Lorraine Hansberry

"*D*on't ever become a pessimist... a

pessimist is correct oftener than an optimist, but an optimist has more fun, and neither can stop the march of events."

- Robert A. Heinlein

"*O*ne must not lose desires. They are

mighty stimulants to creativeness, to love, and to long life."

- Alexander A. Bogomoletz

By Robyna Smith-Keys.

"*T*he hardest arithmetic to master is that which enables us to count our blessings."

- Eric Hoffer

"*H*e who has not looked on sorrow will never see joy."

- Kahlil Gibran

"*T*he happy person is the one who finds occasions for joy at every step. He does not have to look for them, he just finds them."

- Ossian Lang

"*B*e glad of life because it gives you the

chance to love, to work, to play, and to
look up at the stars".

- Henry Van Dyke

"*T*wo men look out through the same bars.

One sees the mud and one the stars."

- Frederick Langbridge

"*S*eek ye first the good things of the

mind, and the rest will either be
supplied or its loss will not be felt."

- Francis Bacon

"*L*earn how to turn frustration into fascination. You will learn more being fascinated by life than you will by being frustrated by it."

- Jim Rohn

"*G*et pleasure out of life...as much as you can. Nobody every died from pleasure."

- Sol Hurok

"*T*he privilege of a lifetime is being who you are."

- Joseph Campbell

"*A*lways laugh when you can.

It is cheap medicine."

— Lord Byron

"*A*nger is only one letter short of

danger."

— Unknown

*H*a Ha Ha

Be Hap Hap Happy
There is nothing to lose.

By Robyna Smith-Keys.

"**R**ealize that true happiness lies

within you. Waste no time and effort
searching for peace and contentment
and joy in the world outside. Remember
that there is no happiness in having or in
getting, but only in giving. Reach out.
Share. Smile. Hug. Happiness is a
perfume you cannot pour on others
without getting a few drops on yourself."

- Og Mandino

"**J**oy is not a thing, it is in us."

- Charles Wagner

"*O*ur greatest happiness does not

depend on the condition of life in which
chance has placed us, but is always the
result of a good conscience, good health,
occupation and freedom in all just
pursuits."

- Thomas Jefferson

"*G*ratitude unlocks the fullness of life.

It turns what we have into enough, and
more. It turns denial into acceptance,
chaos to order, confusion to clarity. It
can turn a meal into a feast, a house into
a home, a stranger into a friend.
Gratitude makes sense of our past,
brings peace for today, and creates a
vision for tomorrow."

- Melody Beattie

"*A*s long as you derive inner help and comfort from anything, keep it."

- Mahatma Gandhi

"*I*f you will call your troubles experiences, and remember that every experience develops some latent force within you, you will grow vigorous and happy, however adverse your circumstances may seem to be."

- John R. Miller

"*T*he joy that isn't shared dies young."

- Anne Sexton

"*I* don't believe people are looking for

the meaning of life as much as they are looking for the experience of being alive."

- Joseph Campbell

"*The* journey between what you once

were and who you are now becoming is where the dance of life really takes place."

- Barbara De Angelis

"*G*rief is the agony of an instant, the

indulgence of grief the blunder of a life."

- Benjamin Disraeli

By Robyna Smith-Keys.

"*T*he truth is that all of us attain the

greatest success and happiness possible
in this life whenever we use our native
capacities to their greatest extent."

- Smiley Blanton

"*W*e act as though comfort and luxury

were the chief requirements of life, when
all that we need to make us happy is
something to be enthusiastic about."

- Charles Kingsley

"*I*t is impossible to live in the past,

difficult to live in the present and a
waste to live in the future."

- Frank Herbert

"*Y*outh is a circumstance you can't do anything about. The trick is to grow up without getting old."

- Frank Lloyd Wright

"*T*oday I choose life. Every morning when I wake up I can choose joy, happiness, negativity, pain ... to feel the freedom that comes from being able to continue to make mistakes and choices. Today I choose to feel life, not to deny my humanity, but embrace it."

- Kevyn Aucoin

By Robyna Smith-Keys.

"*P*eople are always blaming their

circumstances for what they are. I don't
believe in circumstances. The people
who get on in this world are the people
who get up and look for the
circumstances they want, and if they
can't find them, make them."

- George Bernard Shaw

"*T*he greatest revolution of our

generation is the discovery that human
beings, by changing the inner attitudes
of their minds, can change the outer
aspects of their lives."

- William James

188

"*Y*ou are always a valuable, worthwhile

human being; not because anybody says
so, not because you're successful, not
because you make a lot of money, but
because you decide to believe it and for
no other reason."

- Wayne Dyer

"*W*hen you look at your life, the
greatest happinesses,
are family happinesses."

- Joyce Brothers

By Robyna Smith-Keys.

"*H*appiness comes from within. It is

not dependent on external things or on other people. You become vulnerable and can be easily hurt when your feelings of security and happiness depend on the behavior and actions of other people. Never give your power to anyone else."

- Brian L. Weiss

"*E*verything can be taken from a

[person] but one thing: the last of the human freedoms—to choose one's attitude in any given set of circumstances, to choose one's own way."

- Viktor E. Frankl

"*If* you want to find greater happiness

and fulfillment in your life, you must begin to understand and live in harmony with the law of attraction."

- Jack Canfield

"*Death* is not the biggest fear we have;

our biggest fear is taking the risk to be alive, and risking to be alive and express what and who we really are."

- Don Miguel Ruiz

"*The* tragedy of life is not death, but what we let die inside us while we live."

- Native American

By Robyna Smith-Keys.

"*The* secret of happiness is in a cheerful, contented mind. He is poor who is dissatisfied; he is rich who is contented with what he has, and can enjoy what others own."

- Orison Swett Marden

"*A*ssociate only with positive, focused people who you can learn from and who will not drain your valuable energy with uninspiring attitudes. By developing relationships with those committed to constant improvement and the pursuit of the best that life has to offer, you will have plenty of company on your path to the top of whatever mountain you seek to climb."

- Robin Sharma

"*The* positive thinker sees the invisible, feels the intangible, and achieves the impossible."

- Anonymous

"*What* I am suggesting is that each of us turn from the negativism that permeates our society and look for the remarkable good among those with whom we associate, that we speak of one another's virtues more than we speak of one another's faults, that optimism replace pessimism, that our faith exceed our fears. When I was a young man and was prone to speak critically, my father would say: 'Cynics do not contribute, skeptics do not create, doubters do not achieve'."

- Gordon B. Hinckley

"*U*ltimately, contentment is more a shift in attitude than a change in circumstances."

- Linda Dillow

"*Y*ou need to learn how to select your thoughts just the same way you select your clothes every day. This is a power you can cultivate. If you want to control things in your life so bad, work on the mind. That's the only thing you should be trying to control."

- Elizabeth Gilbert

"*T*alking about our problems is our greatest addiction. Break the habit. Talk about your joys."

- Rita Schiano

"*H*appiness is an attitude of mind,

born of the simple determination to be happy under all outward circumstances."

- J. Donald Walters

"*L*ive life fully while you're here.

Experience everything. Take care of yourself and your friends. Have fun, be crazy, be weird. Go out and screw up! You're going to anyway, so you might as well enjoy the process. Take the opportunity to learn from your mistakes: find the cause of your problem and eliminate it. Don't try to be perfect; just be an excellent example of being human."

- Anthony Robbins

By Robyna Smith-Keys.

" *O*ne of the secrets of a happy life is

continuous small treats."

- Iris Murdoch

" *O*ne of the things I learned the hard

way was that it doesn't pay to get
discouraged. Keeping busy and making
optimism a way of life can restore your
faith in yourself."

- Lucille Ball

" *G*ratitude begins where my sense of

entitlement ends."

- Steven Furtick

"*S*ome luck lies in not getting what

you thought you wanted but getting what you have, which once you have got it you may be smart enough to see is what you would have wanted had you known."

- Garrison Keillor

"*Y*our mental attitude is something

you can control outright and you must use self-discipline until you create a Positive Mental Attitude - your mental attitude attracts to you everything that makes you what you are."

- Napoleon Hill

By Robyna Smith-Keys.

"*If* my heart can become pure and

simple like that of a child, I think there probably can be no greater happiness than this."

- Kitaro Nishida

"*What* happens is not as important as how you react to what happens."

- Thaddeus Golas

"*He* who is not contented with what he

has, would not be contented with what he would like to have."

- Socrates

198

"*W*rite it on your heart that every day

is the best day in the year."

- Ralph Waldo Emerson

"*W*e can always find something to be

thankful for, no matter what may be the
burden of our wants, or the special
subject of our petitions."

- Albert Barnes

"*T*here is no sadder sight than a young

pessimist."

- Mark Twain

By Robyna Smith-Keys.

"*H*appiness is like mercury. Hard to

hold, and when we drop it, it shatters
into a million pieces. Maybe the bravest
of all are those who have the courage to
reach for it again."

- Mary Higgins Clark

"*T*hat action is best which procures the

greatest happiness."

- Francis Hutcheson

"*T*he life you are leading is simply a

reflection of your thinking."

- Doug Firebaugh

"*L*ive life fully while you're here.

Experience everything. Take care of yourself and your friends. Have fun, be crazy, be weird. Go out and screw up! You're going to anyway, so you might as well enjoy the process. Take the opportunity to learn from your mistakes: find the cause of your problem and eliminate it. Don't try to be perfect; just be an excellent example of being human."

- Anthony Robbins

"*If* you don't like something, change it. If you can't change it, change your attitude. Don't complain."

- Maya Angelou

By Robyna Smith-Keys.

"*The* happiest people are those who

think the most interesting thoughts.
Those who decide to use leisure as a
means of mental development, who love
good music, good books, good pictures,
good company, good conversation, are
the happiest people in the world. And
they are not only happy in themselves,
they are the cause of happiness in
others."

- William Lyon Phelps

"*I* would maintain that thanks are

the highest form of thought; and that
gratitude is happiness doubled by
wonder."

- G.K. Chesterton

Ba Ha Ha Happy!

"*T*he more you praise and celebrate your life, the more there is in life to celebrate."

- Oprah Winfrey

"*I*t really is easy to forget the unpleasant if we simply refuse to recall it. Withdraw only positive thoughts from your memory bank. Let the others fade away. And your confidence, that feeling of being on top of the world, will zoom up-ward. You take a big step forward toward conquering your fear when you refuse to remember negative, self-deprecating thoughts."

- David J. Schwartz

By Robyna Smith-Keys.

"*P*erfection of character is this: to live

each day as if it were your last, without
frenzy, without apathy, without
pretense."

- Marcus Aurelius

"*I*t is not easy to find happiness in

ourselves, and it is not possible to find it
elsewhere."

- Agnes Repplier

"*A*s we express our gratitude, we must

never forget that the highest
appreciation is not to utter words, but to
live by them."

- John Fitzgerald Kennedy

"*May* your walls know joy; May every

room hold laughter and every window
open to great possibility."

- Maryanne Radmacher-Hershey

"*You* and I do not see things as they

are. We see things as we are."

- Herb Cohen

"*When* we recall Christmas past, we

usually find that the simplest things -
not the great occasions - give off the
greatest glow of happiness."

- Bob Hope

By Robyna Smith-Keys.

"*If* my heart can become pure and

simple like that of a child, I think there probably can be no greater happiness than this."

- Kitaro Nishida

"*E*verything that irritates us about others

can lead us to an understanding of ourselves."

- Carl Gustav Jung

"*At* the end of our time on earth, if we have

lived fully, we will not be able to say, 'I was always happy'. Hopefully we will be able to say, 'I have experienced a lifetime of real moments, and many of them were happy moments.'"

- Barbara DeAngelis

"*S*tress is an ignorant state. It believes

that everything is an emergency.
Nothing is that important."

- Natalie Goldberg

"*G*et pleasure out of life...as much as

you can. Nobody ever died from
pleasure."

- Sol Hurok

"*H*ave a heart that never hardens, and

a temper that never tires, and a touch
that never hurts."

- Charles Dickens

By Robyna Smith-Keys.

"*It* is only by following your deepest

instinct that you can lead a rich life, and
if you let your fear of consequence
prevent you from following your deepest
instinct, then your life will be safe,
expedient and thin."

- Katharine Butler Hathaway

"*He* is a wise man who does not

grieve for the things which he has not,
but rejoices for those which he has."

- Epictetus

"*In* order to live free and happily you

must sacrifice boredom. It is not always
an easy sacrifice."

- Richard Bach

"*G*ratitude makes sense of our past,

brings peace for today, and creates a
vision for tomorrow."

- Melody Beattie

"*At* whatever straws we must grasp,

there is always a time for gratitude and
new beginnings."

- J. Robert Moskin

By Robyna Smith-Keys.

" *W*hat other people think about me is

not my business."

- Michael J. Fox

" *W*hen you relinquish the desire to

control your future, you can have more
happiness."

- Nicole Kidman, in   The Scotsman

" *T*he more you eat, the less flavor; the

less you eat, the more flavor."

- Chinese Proverb

"*I* can think of no better way of

redeeming this tragic world today than love and laughter. Too many of the young have forgotten how to laugh, and too many of the elders have forgotten how to love. Would not our lives be lightened if only we could all learn to laugh more easily at ourselves and to love one another."

- Theodore Hesburgh

"*I*ndolence is a delightful but

distressing state; we must be doing something to be happy."

- Mahatma Gandhi

By Robyna Smith-Keys.

"*T*he good life, as I conceive it, is a

happy life. I do not mean that if you are
good you will be happy - I mean that if
you are happy you will be good."

- Bertrand Russell

"*L*ife begins as a quest of the child for

the man [person] and ends as a journey
by the man [person] to rediscover the
child."

- Laurens Van der Post

"*O*ne thing you can't recycle is wasted

time."

- Anonymous

"*H*appiness and peace of mind are a matter of consciousness. We must create the harmony we desire. As we raise our level of consciousness we become more in tune with the true nature of our being. This type of awareness is not an accident; it comes from study and an understanding that we are truly creative."

- Bob Proctor

"*T*hat action is best which procures the greatest happiness."

- Francis Hutcheson

By Robyna Smith-Keys.

"*F*or myself, I am an optimist - it does

not seem to be much use being anything
else."

- Sir Winston Churchill

"*T*o be without some of the things you

want is an indispensable part of
happiness."

- Bertrand Russell

"*I* never think of the future. It comes

soon enough."

- Albert Einstein

"*A* cloudy day is no match for a sunny disposition."

- William Arthur Ward

"*H*appiness does not come from doing easy work but from the afterglow of satisfaction that comes after the achievement of a difficult task that demanded our best."

- Theodore Isaac Rubin

"*T*he ingredients of health and long life are great temperance, open air, easy labor, and little care."

- Sir Philip Sidney

By Robyna Smith-Keys.

"*A* human being has a natural desire

to have more of a good thing than he
needs."

- Mark Twain

"*N*o pessimist ever discovered the

secret of the stars, or sailed to an
uncharted land, or opened a new
doorway for the human spirit."

- Helen Keller

"*S*ome people walk in the rain; others

just get wet."

- Roger Miller

"*A*s human beings we all want to be

happy and free from misery... we have learned that the key to happiness is inner peace. The greatest obstacles to inner peace are disturbing emotions such as anger, attachment, fear and suspicion, while love and compassion and a sense of universal responsibility are the sources of peace and happiness."

- Dalai Lama

"*T*here is little difference in people, but

that little difference makes a big difference. The little difference is attitude. The big difference is whether it is positive or negative."

- W. Clement Stone

" *O*ur emotions need to be as educated

as our intellect. It is important to know
how to feel, how to respond, and how to
let life in so that it can touch you."

- Jim Rohn

"*T*o insure good health: eat lightly,

breathe deeply, live moderately,
cultivate cheerfulness, and maintain an
interest in life."

- William Londen

"*I*t is difficult for sorrow to intrude on

a busy life."

- Unknown

"*The* pessimist complains about the wind; the optimist expects it to change; the realist adjusts the sails."

- William Arthur Ward

"*A* three-year-old child is a being who gets almost as much fun out of a fifty-six dollar set of swings as it does out of finding a small green worm."

- Bill Vaughan

"*To* be truly happy is a question of how we begin and not of how we end, of what we want and not of what we have."

- Robert Louis Stephenson

By Robyna Smith-Keys.

"*S*top worrying about the potholes in

the road and celebrate the journey!"

- Barbara Hoffman

"*L*aughing deeply is living deeply."

- Milan Kundera

"*A* contented mind is a continual

feast."

- American Proverb

"*B*eautiful things happen when you

distance yourself from the negative."

- Unknown

"*T*his is my wish for you: Comfort on

difficult days, smiles when sadness
intrudes, rainbows to follow the clouds,
laughter to kiss your lips, sunsets to
warm your heart, hugs when spirits sag,
beauty for your eyes to see, friendships
to brighten your being, faith so that you
can believe, confidence for when you
doubt, courage to know yourself,
patience to accept the truth, Love to
complete your life."

- Unknown

By Robyna Smith-Keys.

"*T*here is only one way to happiness

and that is to cease worrying about things which are beyond the power of our will."

- Epictetus

"*M*ost people are searching for

happiness. They're looking for it. They're trying to find it in someone or something outside of themselves. That's a fundamental mistake. Happiness is something that you are, and it comes from the way you think."

- Wayne Dyer

"*D*o not regret growing older. It's a

privilege denied to many.
The wisdom of the years brings
emotional stability."

- Robyna Smith-Keys

"*B*eliefs have the power to create and

the power to destroy. Human beings
have the awesome ability to take any
experience of their lives and create a
meaning that dis-empowers them or one
that can literally save their lives."

- Tony Robbins

By Robyna Smith-Keys.

"*E*nergy is that amazing feeling that

comes to life inside of you when you're
happy and believe in yourself."

- Richard Simmons

"*M*ost fears cannot withstand the test

of careful scrutiny and analysis. When
we expose our fears to the light of
thoughtful examination they usually just
evaporate."

- Jack Canfield

"*T*he tragedy of life is not death, but

what we let die inside us while we live."

- Native American

"*W*e must all suffer from one of two

pains: the pain of discipline or the pain of regret. The difference is discipline weighs ounces while regret weighs tons."

- Jim Rohn

"*A* mother's happiness is like a

beacon, lighting up the future but reflected also on the past in the guise of fond memories."

- Honore de Balzac

By Robyna Smith-Keys.

"*T*he key to life is imagination. If you don't have that, no mater what you have, it's meaningless. If you do have imagination...you can make feast of straw."

- Jane Stanton Hitchcock

"*A*fter all it is those who have a deep and real inner life who are best able to deal with the irritating details of outer life."

- Evelyn Underhill

"*A*void having your ego so close to

your position that when your position
falls, your ego goes with it."

- Colin Powell

"*T*he outer conditions of a person's life

will always be found to reflect their
inner beliefs."

- James Allen

"*E*njoy the little things, for one day you

may look back and realize they were the
big things."

- Robert Brault

By Robyna Smith-Keys.

" *O*ne day at a time - this is enough. Do

not look back and grieve over the past,
for it is gone: and do not be troubled
about the future, for it has not yet come.
Live in the present, and make it so
beautiful that it will be worth
remembering."

- Ida Scott Taylor

" *B*e the person you want to have and

you will find yourself on a path to
ultimate happiness."

-Jordan Canon

Ba Ha Ha Happy!

"*F*ind ecstasy in life - the mere sense of

living is joy enough."

- Emily Dickinson

"*L*ife must be lived as play."

- Plato

"*W*e are most nearly ourselves when

we achieve the seriousness of the child
at play."

- Heraclitus

By Robyna Smith-Keys.

"*N*o matter how old you are, there's always something good to look forward to."

- Lynn Johnston

"*I*f you can walk you can dance, if you can talk you can sing."

- Zimbabwean Proverb

"*M*ake happy those who are near, and those who are far will come."

- Chinese Proverb

"*A*cceptance of what has happened is

the first step to overcoming the
consequences of any misfortune."

- William James

"*B*e the person you want to have in

your life and you will find yourself on a
path to ultimate happiness."

- Jordan Canon

"*T*rue happiness arises, in the first

place, from the enjoyment of one's self."

- Joseph Addison

By Robyna Smith-Keys.

"*E*very person has the power to make

others happy. Some do it simply by
entering a room - others by leaving the
room. Some individuals leave trails of
gloom; others, trails of joy. Some leave
trails of hate and bitterness; others,
trails of love and harmony. Some leave
trails of cynicism and pessimism; others
trails of faith and optimism. Some leave
trails of criticism and resignation; others
trails of gratitude and hope. What kind
of trails do you leave?"

- William Arthur Ward

"*H*appiness and gratitude are inextricably linked; for happiness will rarely if ever come to those who fail to appreciate what they already have."

- Unknown Source

"*H*appiness always looks small while you hold it in your hands, but let it go, and you learn at once how big and precious it is."

- Maxim Gorky

"*A*n act of goodness is of itself an act of happiness. No reward coming after the event can compare with the sweet reward that went with it."

- Maurice Masterlinck

By Robyna Smith-Keys.

"*C*heerfulness keeps up a kind of daylight in the mind, and fills it with a steady and perpetual serenity."

- Joseph Addison

"*B*efore we set our hearts too much on anything, let us examine how happy are those who already possess it."

- La Rochefoucauld

"*I*t's a sign of mediocrity when you demonstrate gratitude with moderation."

- Roberto Benigni

"*T*his is my wish for you:

peace of mind, prosperity through the year, happiness that multiplies, health for you and yours, fun around every corner, energy to chase your dreams, joy to fill your holidays!"

- D.M. Dellinger

"*A* life without a cause is a life without effect."

- Albert Einstein

"*O*n this planet, there are people with talents

and people with flaws. The smart ones learn to
use their talents, but the happy ones learn to
accept their flaws."

- Dick Solomon

"*If* you're able to be yourself, then you

have no competition. All you have to do
is get closer and closer to that essence."

- Barbara Cook

"*T*he more you praise and celebrate

your life, the more there is in life to
celebrate."

- Oprah Winfrey

"*P*eople get so in the habit of worry

that if you save them from drowning and
put them on a bank to dry in the sun
with hot chocolate and muffins they
wonder whether they are catching cold."

- John Jay Chapman

By Robyna Smith-Keys.

" *G*rab the broom of anger and drive off

the beast of fear."

- Zora Neale Hurston

" *T*he way I see it, you should live

everyday like its your birthday."

- Paris Hilton

" *P*eople who live the most fulfilling

lives are the ones who are always

rejoicing at what they have."

- Richard Carlson

"*C*elebrate the happiness that friends
are always giving, make every day a
holiday and celebrate just living!"

- Amanda Bradley

"*G*et the most out of everything in
your life; the happiness and the sadness,
the success and the failure...get a good
perspective of what life is all about. Let
the orchestra of your life play all the
notes, the high notes, the low rumblings
of the difficulties and perplexities that
all we all face."

- Jim Rohn

By Robyna Smith-Keys.

"*W*e take greater pains to persuade

others that we are happy

than in endeavoring to think so
ourselves."

- Confucius

"*H*appiness can be defined, in part at

least, as the fruit of the desire and ability
to sacrifice what we want now for what
we want eventually."

- Stephen Covey

" *Y*ou can never get enough of what you

don't really need."

- Eric Hoffer

" *V*iew change as the one constant in

your life. Welcome it. Expect it.
Anticipate it."

- Colby Fox

" *I*n every real [person] a child is

hidden that wants to play."

- Friedrich Wilhelm Nietzsche

By Robyna Smith-Keys.

" *M*ost [people] pursue pleasure with

such breathless haste that they hurry
past it."

- Kierkegaard

" *Y*ou'll seldom experience regret for

anything that you've done. It is what you
haven't done that will torment you. The
message, therefore, is clear. Do it!
Develop an appreciation for the present
moment. Seize every second of your life
and savor it. Value your present
moments. Using them up in any self-
defeating ways means you've lost them
forever."

- Wayne Dyer

"*If* you look at what you have in life,

you'll always have more. If you look at what you don't have in life, you'll never have enough."

- Oprah Winfrey

"*Be* thankful for what you have; you'll

end up having more. If you concentrate on what you don't have, you will never, ever have enough."

- Oprah Winfrey

"*I* would maintain that thanks are the

highest form of thought, and that
gratitude is happiness doubled by
wonder."

- Gilbert Keith Chesterton

"*G*ratitude helps you to grow and

expand; gratitude brings joy and
laughter into your life and into the lives
of all those around you."

- Eileen Caddy

"*I*t is impossible to feel grateful and

depressed in the same moment."

- Naomi Williams

"*T*he reason people find it so hard to

be happy is that they always see the past
better than it was, the present worse
than it is, and the future less resolved
than it will be."

- Marcel Pagnol

"*T*he only person you are destined to

become is the person YOU DECIDE to
be."

- Ralph Waldo Emerson

By Robyna Smith-Keys.

"*If* you wish to achieve worthwhile

things in your personal and career life,
you must be a worthwhile person in your
own self-development".

- Brian Tracy

"*Attaining* lasting happiness requires

that we enjoy the journey on our way

toward a destination we deem valuable.

Happiness is not about making it to the

peak of the mountain nor is it about

climbing aimlessly around the

mountain; happiness is the experience

of climbing toward the peak."

- Tal Ben

"*N*ow is no time to think of what you

do not have. Think of what you can do
with what there is."

- Ernest Hemingway

"*N*ever let your persistence and

passion turn into stubbornness and
ignorance."

- Anthony D'Angelo

"*N*o pessimist ever discovered the

secrets of the stars, or sailed to
uncharted land, or opened a new
doorway for the human spirit."

- Helen Keller

"*T*he greatest revelation of my life is the

discovery that individuals can change
the outer aspects of their lives by
changing the inner attitudes of their
minds."

- William James

"*R*eal, constructive mental power lies

in the creative thought that shapes your
destiny, and your hour-by-hour mental
conduct produces power for change in
your life. Develop a train of thought on
which to ride. The nobility of your life as
well as your happiness depends upon
the direction in which that train of
thought is going."

- Laurence J. Peter

"*T*he voyage of discovery is not in seeking new landscapes but in having new eyes."

- Marcel Proust

" *G*ratitude unlocks the fullness of life. It turns what we have into enough, and more. It turns denial into acceptance, chaos to order, confusion to clarity. It can turn a meal into a feast, a house into a home, a stranger into a friend. Gratitude makes sense of our past, brings peace for today, and creates a vision for tomorrow."

- Melody Beattie

By Robyna Smith-Keys.

"*I*believe in the sun, even when it
rains."

- Anne Frank

"*T*he habit of giving only enhances the
desire to give."

- Walt Whitman

"*T*he cave you fear to enter holds the
treasure you seek."

- Joseph Campbell

"*T*here is only one blasphemy, and that is the refusal to experience joy."

- Paul Rudnick

"*T*ime is a flowing river. Happy are those who allow themselves to be carried, unresisting, with the current. They float through easy days. They live, unquestioning, in the moment."

- Christopher Darlington Morley

"*T*he most wasted of all days is one without laughter."

- E.E. Cummings

By Robyna Smith-Keys.

"*I*ve grown to realize the joy that

comes from little victories is preferable
to the fun that comes from ease and the
pursuit of pleasure."

- Lawana Blackwell

"*H*appiness comes when you believe in

what you are doing, know what you are
doing, and love what you are doing."

- Brian Tracy

"*D*on't worry about anything.

Worrying never solved anything. All it
does is distort your mind."

- Milton Garland

"*Y*ou don't stop laughing because you grow old. You grow old because you stop laughing."

- Michael Pritchard

"*H*appiness comes of the capacity to feel deeply, to enjoy simply, to think freely, to risk life, to be needed."

- Storm Jameson

"*L*earn to be calm and you will always be happy."

- Paramahansa Yogananda

By Robyna Smith-Keys.

"*The* satisfaction that accompanies good acts is itself not the motivation of the act; satisfaction is not the motive, but only the consequence."

- Bishop Joseph Butler

"*Never* feel self-pity, the most destructive emotion there is. How awful to be caught up in the terrible squirrel cage of self."

- Millicent Fenwick

"*Nurture* your mind with great thoughts."

- Benjamin Disraeli

"*You* cannot control what happens to

you, but you can control your attitude toward what happens to you, and in that, you will be mastering change rather than allowing it to master you."

- Brian Tracy

"*When* you change the way you look

at things, the things you look at change."

- Wayne Dyer

"*Our* ultimate freedom is the right and

power to decide how anybody or anything outside ourselves will affect us."

- Stephen Covey

By Robyna Smith-Keys.

"*It's* not what's happening to you now

or what has happened in your past that
determines who you become. Rather, it's
your decisions about what to focus on,
what things mean to you, and what
you're going to do about them that will
determine your ultimate destiny."

- Anthony Robbins

"*May* you live every day of your life."

- Jonathan Swift

"*L*earn to see in another's calamity the

ills which you should avoid."

- Publilius Syrus

"*T*he key to human happiness lies

within our own state of mind, and so too
do the primary obstacles to that
happiness."

- Dalai Lama

"*T*here is always something for which to

be thankful."

- Charles Dickens

By Robyna Smith-Keys.

"*L*ike a fragrance to a flower, true

happiness is an expression of your
unconditional self...the real you."

- Robert Holden

"*W*e can gradually grow into any

condition we desire, provided we first
make ourselves in habitual mental
attitude the person who corresponds to
those conditions."

- Thomas Troward

"*E*very human being is the author of

his own health or disease."

- Buddha

"*Y*our present circumstances don't

determine where you can go; they
merely determine where you start."

- Nido Qubein

"*E*very human being is the author of

his own health or disease."

- Buddha

"*U*ntil you are happy with who you

are, you will never be happy with what
you have."

- Zig Ziglar

By Robyna Smith-Keys.

"*N*obody can go back and start a new

beginning, but anyone can start today
and make a new ending."

- Maria Robinson

"*T*here is no way to happiness.

Happiness is the way."

- Buddha

"*T*he clearest sign of wisdom is

continued cheerfulness."

- Michel Eyquem de Montaigne

"*B*asically, you can live your life in one

of two ways. You can let your brain run you the way it has in the past. You can let it flash any picture or sound or feeling, and you can respond automatically on cue, like a Pavlovian dog responding to a bell. Or you can choose to consciously run your brain yourself. You can implant the cues you want. You can take bad experiences and sap them of their strength and power. You can represent them to yourself in a way that no longer overpowers you, a way that "cuts them down" to a size where you know you can effectively handle things."

- Anthony Robbins

By Robyna Smith-Keys.

"*N*ever limit your view of life by any

past experience."

- Ernest Holmes

"*H*appiness can be defined, in part at

least, as the fruit of the desire and ability
to sacrifice what we want now for what
we want eventually".

- Stephen Covey

"*S*mile a lot. Not only will you turn

heads, you'll turn hearts."

- Andrea Oldham

"*I*t isn't what you have, or who you are, or where you are, or what you are doing that makes you happy or unhappy. It is what you think about."

- Dale Carnegie

"*T*he reason people find it so hard to be happy is that they always see the past better than it was, the present worse than it is, and the future less resolved than it will be."

- Marcel Pagnol

"*I*t is the way we react to circumstances that determines our feelings."

- Dale Carnegie

263

By Robyna Smith-Keys.

"*W*e all live with the objective of being happy, our lives are all different and yet the same."

- Anne Frank

"*A*ffirm continuously to yourself: I am in the right place, at the right time, for the right purpose."

- Ursula Roberts

"*Y*our attitude is the hinge upon which the door of your destiny swings."

- Keith Craft

" *Y*our living is determined not so much by what life brings to you as by the attitude you bring to life; not so much by what happens to you as by the way your mind looks at what happens."

- Kahlil Gibran

"*T*he way I see it if you want the rainbow you gotta put up with the rain."

- Dolly Parton

"*L*ife is a continuous exercise in creative problem solving."

- Michael J. Gelb

By Robyna Smith-Keys.

"*T*o avoid criticism do nothing, say

nothing, be nothing."

- Elbert Hubbard

"*T*he truth you believe and cling to

makes you unavailable to hear

anything new."

- Chodrun

"*H*appiness is not a future event."

- Joe Fortenberry

"*N*o day in which you learn something

is a complete loss."

- David Eddings

"*E*motions will either serve or master,

depending on who is in charge."

- Jim Rohn

"*H*appiness is like those palaces in

fairy tales whose gates are guarded by
dragons; we must fight in order to
conquer it."

- Alexandre Dumas

By Robyna Smith-Keys.

"*L*ive with passion!"

- Tony Robbins

"*W*hen someone does something

good, applaud. You will make two
people happy."

- Samuel Goldwyn

"*N*ever underestimate the power of

passion."

- Eve Sawyer

"*W*anting ... is something 'having'

cannot cure."

- Joe Fortenberry

"*S*ome cause happiness wherever they

go; others whenever they go."

- Oscar Wilde

"*Y*ou just have to do your own thing,

no matter what anyone says. It's your
life."

- Ethan Embry

By Robyna Smith-Keys.

"*If* you want to live a happy life, tie it

to a goal, not to people or things."

- Albert Einstein

"*Blessed* is he who expects nothing,

for he shall never be disappointed."

- Alexander Pope

"*Imagine* every day to be the last of a

life surrounded with hopes, cares, anger,
and fear. The hours that come
unexpectedly will be so much more the
grateful."

- Horace

"*A*ny fool can criticize, condemn, and

complain - and most fools do."

— Dale Carnegie

"*T*he major cause of stress is the

inability of people to discover their true
nature. Discover your gifts, follow them
and you will never feel stressed."

— Pavel Stoyanov

"*H*umanity does not ask us to be

happy. It merely asks us to be brilliant
on its behalf. Survival first, then
happiness as we can manage it."

— Orson Scott Card

By Robyna Smith-Keys.

"*T*here is nothing that wastes the body
like worry".

- Mohandas Gandhi

"*H*appiness comes of the capacity to

feel deeply, to enjoy simply, to think
freely, to risk life, to be needed".

- Storm Jameson

"*Y*ou don't get ulcers from what you

eat, you get them from what's eating
you".

- Vicki Baum

"One of the secrets of a happy life is continuous small treats."

- Iris Murdoch

"Abiding happiness is not simply a possibility, but a duty all may live above the troubles of life worry is a poison and happiness is a medicine."

- Newell Dwight Hillis

"Adopting the right attitude can convert a negative stress into a positive one."

- Dr. Hans Selye

By Robyna Smith-Keys.

"*If* you want to turn your life around,

try thankfulness. It will change your life
mightily."

- Gerald Good

"*We* often take for granted the very

things that most deserve our gratitude."

- Cynthia Ozick

"*Real* life isn't always going to be

perfect or go our way, but the recurring
acknowledgement of what is working in
our lives can help us not only to survive
but surmount our difficulties."

- Sara Ban Breathnach

" *G*ifts of time and love are surely the

basic ingredients of a truly merry
Christmas."

- Peg Bracken

" *N*ever limit your view of life by any

past experience."

- Ernest Holmes

" *If* you want your life to be more

rewarding, you have to change the way
you think."

- Oprah Winfrey

"*W*hen you cease to make a contribution you begin to die."

- Roosevelt, Eleanor

"*I*f you take care of the small things, the big things take care of themselves. You can gain more control over your life by paying closer attention to the little things."

- Emily Elizabeth Dickinson

"*L*ive to the point of tears."

- Albert Camus

"*B*e able to be alone. Lose not the
advantage of solitude, and the society of
thyself."

- Sir Thomas Browne

"*G*reat anger is more destructive than
the sword."

- Tamil Proverb

"*Y*ou can either hold yourself up to the
unrealistic standards of others, or ignore
them and concentrate on being happy
with yourself as you are."

- J. Jacques

By Robyna Smith-Keys.

"*A* day of worry is more exhausting
than a week of work."

> - John Lubbock

"*H*appiness can be defined, in part at
least, as the fruit of the desire and ability
to sacrifice what we want now for what
we want eventually".

> - Stephen Covey

"*T*he worst thing you can possibly do is
worrying and thinking about what you
could have done."

> - Georg Christoph Lichtenberg

"*T*here are two primary choices in life:
to accept conditions as they exist,
or accept the responsibility for
changing them."

- Denis Waitley

"*W*rite it on your heart that every day

is the best day in the year."

- Ralph Waldo Emerson

"*D*on't envy for what people have and

you don't. You have something they
don't have."

- Wilson Kanadi

By Robyna Smith-Keys.

"*W*here we have strong emotions, we

are liable to fool ourselves."

- Carl Sagan

"*T*he remarkable thing about the

human mind is its range of limitations."

- Celia Green

"*B*e content with what you have;

rejoice in the way things are. When you
realize there is nothing lacking, the
whole world opens up to you."

- Lao Tzu

"*H*appiness is often the result of being

too busy to be miserable."

- Frank Baer

"*E*verything is passing ... enjoy its

momentariness".

- Mooji

"*T*he greatest happiness is to transform

one's feelings into action."

- Madame de Stael

By Robyna Smith-Keys.

" *O*ther people do not have to change for us to
experience peace of mind."

- Gerald Jampolsky

"*H*appiness is a choice that requires effort at
times."

- Aeschylus

"*T*he worst thing you can try to do is
cling to something that is gone, or to
recreate it."

- Johnette Napolitano

"*D*on't worry, be happy."

\- Bobby McFerrin

"*O*ur attitude toward life determines
life's attitude toward us."

\- Earl Nightingale

"*Y*our life is what your thoughts make
it."

\- Anais Nin

By Robyna Smith-Keys.

"*T*o live is the rarest thing in the world.

Most people exist, that is all."

- Osacar Wilde

"*N*othing can bring you happiness but

yourself."

- Ralph Waldo Emerson

"*D*reams are necessary to life."

- Anais Nin

"*R*emember that the happiest people

are not those getting more, but those giving more."

- H. Jackson Brown, Jr.

"*If* you see ten troubles coming down

the road, you can be sure that nine will run into the ditch before they reach you."

- Calvin Coolidge

"*H*appiness is not something you

postpone for the future; it is something you design for the present."

- Jim Rohn

By Robyna Smith-Keys.

"*D*on't cry because it's over. Smile

because it happened."

- Dr. Seuss

*L*aughter is an instant vacation."

- Milton Berle

"*H*appiness is not a matter of good

fortune or worldly possessions. It's a
mental attitude. It comes from
appreciating what we have, instead of
being miserable about what we don't
have. It's so simple, yet so hard for the
human mind to comprehend."

- Bits and Pieces

"*True* happiness comes from the joy of deeds well done, the zest of creating things new."

- Antoine de Saint-Exupery

"*Never* regret. If it's good, it's wonderful. If it's bad, it's experience."

- Victoria Holt

"*Do* not anticipate trouble, or worry about what may never happen."

- Benjamin Franklin

By Robyna Smith-Keys.

"*S*ometimes when people are under

stress, they hate to think, and it's the
time when they most need to think."

- Bill Clinton

"*B*e content with what you have;

rejoice in the way things are. When you
realize there is nothing lacking, the
world belongs to you."

- Lao Tzu

"*D*o not dwell in the past; do not dream of the future; concentrate the mind on the present moment."

- Buddha

"*L*earn to value yourself, which means: fight for your happiness."

- Ayn Rand

"*O*ne way to get the most out of life is to look upon it as a great adventure."

- William Feather

By Robyna Smith-Keys.

" *W*hy not learn to enjoy the little things? There are so many of them."

- Unknown

" *H*appiness is the meaning and the purpose of life, the whole aim and end of human existence"

- Aristotle

" *R*emember that the happiest people are not those getting more, but those giving more."

- H. Jackson Brown, Jr.

Ba Ha Ha Happy!

"*H*olding on to anger is like grasping a

hot coal with the intent of throwing it at
someone else; you are the one who gets
burned."

- Buddha

"*I*t's not what you look at that matters.

It's what you see."

- Henry David Thoreau

"*I* am more and more convinced that

our happiness or our unhappiness
depends far more on the way we meet
the events of life than on the nature of
those events themselves."

- Karl Wilhelm von Humboldt

By Robyna Smith-Keys.

"*D*on't wait around for other people to

be happy for you. Any happiness you get
you've got to make yourself."

- Alice Walker

"*T*here can be no happiness if the things

we believe in are different from the
things we do."

- Freya Stark

"*I*t is not easy to find happiness in

ourselves, and it is not possible to find it
elsewhere."

- Agnes Repplier

" *You*'ve got to dance like nobody's watching and love like it is never going to hurt."

- Ann Wells

" *A* happy person is not a person in a certain set of circumstances, but rather a person with a certain set of attitudes."

- Hugh Downs

" *It*'s not what you look at that matters, it's what you see."

- Henry David Thoreau

By Robyna Smith-Keys.

"*E*ach of us tends to think we see

things as they are, that we are objective.
But this is not the case. We see the
world, not as it is, but as we are - or as
we are conditioned to see it."

- Stephen Covey

"*S*ometimes the most urgent thing you

can do is take a complete rest."

- Ashleigh Brilliant

"*T*ake control of your emotions, before
your emotions take control of you."

- Scott Dye

"*B*e a fountain, not a drain."

- Rex Hudler

"*T*here is no happiness except in the realization that we have accomplished something."

- Henry Ford

"*T*here are three ingredients to the good life: learning, earning, and yearning."

- Christopher Morley

By Robyna Smith-Keys.

"*The* art of living lies less in eliminating our

troubles than in growing with them."

- Bernard M. Baruch

"*It* is the ability to take a joke, not

make one, that proves you have a sense
of humor."

- Max Eastman

"*The* art of being wise is knowing what

to overlook."

- William James

Ba Ha Ha Happy!

"*L*ife must be lived as play."

- Plato

"*D*o not dwell in the past, do not dream of

the future, concentrate the mind on the present
moment."

- Buddha

" *W*orry is a thin stream of fear tricking

through the mind. If encouraged, it cuts a
channel into which all other thoughts are
drained."

- Arthur Somers Rache

"*E*verywhere you go, take a smile with

you."

- Sasha Azevedo

"*H*appiness does not depend on

outward things, but on the way we see
them."

- Leo Tolstoy

"*H*appiness is: looking in the mirror

and liking what you see."

- Unknown

*G*od Grant Me The Courage

To Change The Things I Can

The Serenity To Accept The Things

I Cannot Change

And The Wisdom

To Know The Difference

AA

"*H*appiness depends more on the inward disposition of the mind than on outward circumstances."

- Benjamin Franklin

"*W*rinkles should merely indicate where smiles have been."

- Mark Twain

By Robyna Smith-Keys.

"**K**nowledge of what is possible is the

beginning of happiness."

- George Santayana

"**T**here is no wealth but life."

- John Ruskin

"**F**eelings change – memories don't."

- Joel Alexander

"*When* the best things are not possible,

the best may be made of those that are."

- Richard Hooker

"*Worrying* is like a rocking chair, it

gives you something to do, but it gets

you nowhere."

- Glenn Turner

"*It's* not work that kills [people], it is

worry."

- Henry Ward Beecher

"*H*appy are those who find fault with themselves instead of finding fault with others."

- Muhammed

"*T*he happiness of most people is not ruined by great catastrophes or fatal errors, but by the repetition of slowly destructive little things."

- Ernest Dimnet

"*A*nger is never without reason, but seldom with a good one."

- Benjamin Franklin

"*The* truth is we can learn to condition

our minds, bodies, and emotions to link
pain and pleasure to whatever we
choose. By changing what we link pain
and pleasure to, we will instantly change
our behaviors."

- Tony Robbins

"*Do* not speak of your happiness to
one less fortunate than yourself."

- Plutarch

"*Only* a few things are really
important."

- Marie Dressler

"*T*here is only one cause of unhappiness: the false beliefs you have in your head; beliefs so widespread, so commonly held, that it never occurs to you to question them."

- Anthony de Mello

"*T*he walls we build around us to keep sadness out also keep out the joy."

- Jim Rohn

"*L*ife consists not in holding good cards but in playing those you hold well."

- Josh Billings

"*H*appiness comes of the capacity to

feel deeply, to enjoy simply, to think freely, to risk life, to be needed."

- Storm Jameson

"*T*he only thing to fear is, fear itself."

- Franklin D. Roosevelt

"*N*ever regret. If it's good, it's wonderful. If it's bad, it's an experience."

- Victoria Holt

"*I* love life because what more is

there?"

- Anthony Hopkins

"*E*very [person] should be born again

on the first day of January.
Start with a fresh page.
Take up one hole more in the buckle if
necessary, or let down one, according to
circumstances; but on the first of
January let every man gird himself once
more, with his face to the front, and take
no interest in the things that were and
are past."

- Henry Ward Beecher

306

"*H*appiness is not a destination; it is a method of life."

- Burton Hills

"*H*appiness is an attitude. We either make ourselves miserable, or happy and strong. The amount of work is the same."

- Francesca Reigler

"*T*he remarkable thing is, we have a choice everyday regarding the attitude we will embrace for that day."

- Charles Swindoll

By Robyna Smith-Keys.

"*T*here is no psychiatrist in the world

like a puppy licking your face."

- Ben Williams

"*A*nd when it rains on your parade,

look up instead of down. Without the
rain, there would be no rainbow."

- Jerry Chin

"*A* mind always employed is always

happy. This is the true secret, the grand
recipe, for felicity."

- Thomas Jefferson

"*P*eople take different roads seeking

fulfillment and happiness. Just because
they are not on your road doesn't mean
they've gotten lost."

- H. Jackson Browne

"*T*hink of all the beauty still left around

you and be happy."

- Anne Frank

"*W*orry bankrupts the spirit."

- Berri Clove

By Robyna Smith-Keys.

"*T*he life of inner peace, being

harmonious and without stress, is the
easiest type of existence."

- Norman Vincent Peale

"*H*appiness is a state of activity."

- Aristotle

"*A*lways do right – it will gratify some

and astonish the rest."

- Mark Twain

"*E*ighty percent of life's satisfaction comes from meaningful relationships."

— Brian Tracy

"*T*o be interested in the changing seasons is a happier state of mind than to be hopelessly in love with spring."

— George Santayana

"*P*eople don't notice whether it's winter or summer when they're happy."

— Anton Chekhov

By Robyna Smith-Keys.

"*W*hen anger rises, think of the

consequences."

- Confucius

"*A*ttitudes are contagious. Make yours

worth catching."

- Unknown Author

"*G*reat effort from great motives is the

best definition of a happy life."

- William Ellery Channing

"*If* something is wrong, fix it if you

can. But train yourself not to worry.
Worry never fixes anything."

- Ernest Hemingway

"*Be* happy. It's one way of being wise."

- Colette

"*As* we express our gratitude, we must

never forget that the highest
appreciation is not to utter words, but to
live by them."

- John Fitzgerald Kennedy

By Robyna Smith-Keys.

" *O*ur happiness depends on wisdom

all the way."

- Sophocles

" *T*he happiness of most people is not

ruined by great catastrophes or fatal
errors, but by the repetition of slowly
destructive little things."

- Ernest Dimnet

" *E*ven a happy life cannot be without a

measure of darkness, and the word
happy would lose its meaning if it were
not balanced by sadness."

- Carl Jung

"*T*he best way to cheer yourself up is to try to cheer somebody else up."

- Mark Twain

"*H*appiness is a direction, not a place."

- Sydney J. Harris

"*I*n our daily lives, we must see that it is not happiness that makes us grateful, but the gratefulness that makes us happy."

- Albert Clarke

By Robyna Smith-Keys.

"*If* you can't sleep, then get up and do

something instead of lying there
worrying. It is the worry that gets you,
not the lack of sleep."

- Dale Carnegie

"*If* you don't like something, change it.

If you can't change it, then change the
way you think about it."

- Mary Englebreit

"*A*lways laugh when you can. It is

cheap medicine."

- Lord Byron

"*H*appiness is a by-product of an effort

to make someone else happy."

- Gretta Brooker Palmer

"*P*ressure is a word that is misused in

our vocabulary. When you start thinking
of pressure, it's because you've started to
think of failure."

- Tommy Lasorda

"*H*appiness and sadness run parallel

to each other. When one takes a rest, the
other one tends to take up the slack."

- Hazelmarie Elliott

By Robyna Smith-Keys.

"*T*here is no cosmetic for beauty like

happiness."

- Lady Blessington

"*T*he greatest weapon against stress is

our ability to choose one thought over
another."

- William James

"*B*eing on top of the world doesn't

mean anything unless you know what
it's like to be at the bottom."

- Rachel Smith

"*W*e are shaped by our thoughts; we become what we think. When the mind is pure, joy follow like a shadow that never leaves".

- Buddha

"*H*appy are those who dream dreams and are ready to pay the price to make them come true."

- Leon J. Suenes

"*F*ind out who you are and do it on purpose."

- Dolly Parton

By Robyna Smith-Keys.

"*H*umor is a means of obtaining

pleasure in spite of the distressing
effects that interface with it."

- Sigmund Freud

"*U*nhappiness is not knowing what we

want and killing ourselves to get it."

- Don Herold

"*I*t is not the place, nor the condition,

but the mind alone that can make
anyone happy or miserable."

- Sir Roger L'Estrange

" *My* personal belief is that the only

thing keeping you from freedom is all
the beliefs you have about what has to
happen before you can be there."

- Tony Robbins

" *A* [person] who suffers or stresses

before it is necessary, suffers more than
is necessary."

- Seneca

" *Attitude* is a little thing that makes a

big difference."

By Robyna Smith-Keys.

- Winston Churchill

" **D**on't let your mind bully your body

into believing it must carry the burden
of its worries."

- Astrid Alauda

" **F**eelings are much like waves, we

can't stop them from coming but we can
choose which one to surf."

- Jonatan Martensson

" *To* be upset over what you don't have

is to waste what you do have."

- Ken S. Keyes, Jr.

" *Wherever* you go, no matter what
the weather, always bring your own
sunshine."

- Anthony J. D'Angelo

" *Gratitude* is riches. Complaint is

poverty."

- Doris Day

By Robyna Smith-Keys.

"*R*emember the past, plan for the

future, but live for today, because
yesterday is gone and tomorrow may
never come."

- Luke

"*Y*ou are only young once, but you can

be immature forever."

- Hannah Marks

"*L*ife may not be the party we hoped

for, but while we are here we might
as well dance."

- Robin Hood

"*L*ive a good, honorable life. Then

when you get older and think back,
you'll be able to enjoy it a second time."

- The Dalai Lama

"*S*ometimes we just need to write

down the good and bad things in life. If
you believe in yourself the good things
will double and the bad things will not."

- Betsey Bosserman Giammattei

"*A* smile will gain you ten more years

of life."

- Chinese Proverb

By Robyna Smith-Keys.

"*H*appiness is neither virtue nor
pleasure, not this thing nor that, but
simply growth."

- W.B.Yeats

Reading Shakespear's

"The stroke of death is as a lovers pinch,

Which hurts and is desired"

From Antony & Cleopatra (Act 5, Scene 5)

 I remembered "Yet each man kills the

thing he loves" from Oscar Wilde...

"*W*e hold these truths to be self-evident, that all men are created equal, that they are endowed by their Creator with certain unalienable rights, that among these are life, liberty and the pursuit of happiness."

- Thomas Jefferson (U.S. Declaration of Independence)

"*I*t is impossible to walk rapidly and be unhappy."

- Howard Murray

"*W*e do not see things as they are. We see them as we are."

- The Talmud

"*T*oo many of us are not living our
dreams because we are living our fears."

- Les Brown

"*W*hat a man is contributes much
more to his happiness than what he has,
or how he is regarded by others."

- Arthur Schopenhauer

"*T*he greatest weapon against stress is
our ability to choose one thought over
another."

- William James

"*If* you don't like something change it; if you can't change it, change the way you think about it."

- Mary Engelbreit

"*The* greatest discovery of my generation is that a person can alter his life by altering his attitude."

- William James

"*You* live longer once you realize that any time spent being unhappy is wasted."

- Ruth E. Renkl

By Robyna Smith-Keys.

"*The* only thing over which you have

complete right of control at all times is
your mental attitude."

- Napoleon Hill

"*It's* only when we truly know and

understand that we have a limited time
on earth - and that we have no way of
knowing when our time is up - that we
will begin to live each day to the fullest,
as if it was the only one we had."

- Elisabeth Kubler-Ross

"*The* most wasted of all days is one

without laughter."

- E.E. Cummings

"*I* don't believe people are looking for

the meaning of life as much as they are
looking for the experience of being
alive."

- Joseph Campbell

"*L*ife isn't about waiting for the storm

to pass...it's about learning to dance in
the rain".

- Unknown Author

"*H*e who has felt the deepest grief is

best able to experience supreme
happiness."

- Alexandre Dumas

"*A*t the end of the day, the key to

happiness is taking ultimate
responsibility for your reactions to all of
your experiences - the good and the
chaotic."

- Yehuda Berg

"*I*t's in your moments of decision that

your destiny is shaped."

- Tony Robbins

Ba Ha Ha Happy!

"*T*he larger the island of knowledge,

the longer the shoreline of wonder."

- Ralph W. Sockman

"*I*f we are to reach real peace in this

world, we shall have to begin with the
children."

- Gandhi

"*M*ix a little foolishness with your

prudence; it's good to be silly at the right
moment."

- Horace

By Robyna Smith-Keys.

"*H*appiness is a continuation of

happenings which are not resisted."

      - Deepak Chopra

"*W*hen guilt rears its ugly head

confront it, discuss it and let it go. The
past is over. It is time to ask what can we
do right, not what did we do wrong.
Forgive yourself and move on."

      - Bernie S. Siegel

"*T*o live is the rarest thing in the world.

Most people exist, that is all."

      - Oscar Wilde

"*A*ct happy, feel happy, be happy,

without a reason in the world. Then you can love, and do what you will."

- Dan Millman

"*I*t isn't the big pleasures that count

the most; it's making a great deal out of the little ones."

- Jean Webster

"*R*egret for the things we did can be

tempered by time; it is regret for the things we did not do that is inconsolable."

- Sydney J. Harris

By Robyna Smith-Keys.

"*F*eelings are determined by how one chooses to respond to various situations and events."

- Ralph Marston

"*Y*our living is determined not so much by what life brings to you as by the attitude you bring to life; not so much by what happens to you as by the way your mind looks at what happens."

- John Homer Miller

"*T*o be happy, make other people happy."

- W. Clement Stone

"*I* love those who can smile in trouble,

who can gather strength from distress,
and grow brave by reflection."

- Leonardo da Vinci

"*B*e glad of life because it gives you the

chance to love and to work and to play
and to look up at the stars."

- Henry Van Dyke

"*T*he place to be happy is here, the time

to be happy is now."

- Robert Ingersoll

By Robyna Smith-Keys.

"*T*he happy people are those who are

producing something; the bored people
are those who are consuming much and
producing nothing."

- William Ralph Inge

"*O*nly passion, great passion, can

elevate the soul to great things."

- Diderot

"*I*f you haven't the strength to impose

your own terms upon life, you must
accept the terms it offers you."

- T.S. Eliot

" Reflect upon your present blessings, of which every [person] has many - not on your past misfortunes, of which all [people] have some."

- Charles Dickens

" Feelings are not controlled by one's circumstances. Feelings are determined by how one choose to respond to various situations and events."

- Ralph Marston

" In the end, it's not the years in your life that count. It's the life in your years."

- Abraham Lincoln

By Robyna Smith-Keys.

" *The* Grand essentials of happiness

are: something to do, something to love,
and something to hope for."

- Allan K. Chalmers

" *Human* beings, by changing the inner

attitudes of their minds, can change the
outer aspects of their lives."

- William James

" *One* way to get the most out of life is

to look upon it as an adventure."

- William Feather

"*L*ive your life each day as you would climb a mountain. An occasional glance towards the summit keeps the goal in mind, but many beautiful scenes are to be observed from each new vantage point."

- Harold B. Melchart

"*T*here is no happiness except in the realization that we have accomplished something."

- Henry Ford

"*I*t makes no difference how many peaks you reach if there was no pleasure in the climb."

- Oprah Winfrey

By Robyna Smith-Keys.

" *B*elieve in yourself! Have faith in your abilities! Without a humble but reasonable confidence in your own powers you cannot be successful or happy."

- Norman Vincent Peale

" *W*e don't always know what makes us happy. We know, instead, what we think SHOULD. We are baffled and confused when our attempts at happiness fail..."

- Julie Cameron

" *W*e don't see things as they are. We see things as we are."

- Annais Nin

"*It* isn't the big pleasures that count

the most; it's making a great deal out of the little ones."

- Jean Webster

"*Our* lives improve only when we take

chances - and the first and most difficult risk we can take is to be honest with ourselves."

- Walter Anderson

"*Love* never fails, character never

quits, and dreams do come true."

– Pete Maravich

343

By Robyna Smith-Keys.

" *M*ay the best things that happened to

you in [last year] be the worst things
that happen to you [this year]."

- Neil J. Cantor

" *R*eflect upon your present blessings,

of which every [person] has many - not
on your past misfortunes, of which all
[people] have some."

- Charles Dickens

" *I*f at first you don't succeed, think

how many people you've made happy."

- H. Duane Black

344

"*T*he road to happiness lies in two simple principles: find what it is that interests you and that you can do well, and when you find it, put your whole soul into it - every bit of energy and ambition and natural ability you have."

- John D. Rockefeller III

"*T*he best and most beautiful things in the world cannot be seen or even touched. They must be felt with the heart. Wishing you happiness."

- Helen Keller

By Robyna Smith-Keys.

" *H*appiness often sneaks in through a

door you didn't know you left open."

- John Barrymore

" *H*ope is itself a species of happiness,

and, perhaps, the chief happiness which
the world affords."

- Samuel Johnson

"*H*appy is the person who knows what

to remember of the past, what to enjoy
in the present, and what to plan for in
the future."

- Arnold Glasgow

"*T*he best way to cheer yourself up is to try to cheer someone else up."

- Mark Twain

"*T*he best and most beautiful things in the world cannot be seen or even touched. They must be felt with the heart. Wishing you happiness."

- Helen Keller

"*A* Definition of Jealousy: The illogical consideration that someone else's success equates to your failure." - Kenneth H. Kaufman

347

"*T*hink of all the beauty still

around you and be happy"

- Anne Frank

"*A*ll that we are is the result of what
we have thought. If a man speaks or acts
with an evil thought, pain follows him. If
a man speaks or acts with a pure
thought, happiness follows him, like a
shadow that never leaves him."

- Buddha

"*C*onfidence on the outside begins by

living with integrity on the inside."

- Brian Tracy

"*L*earn to enjoy every minute of your

life. Be happy now. Don't wait for something outside of yourself to make you happy in the future. Think how really precious is the time you have to spend, whether it's at work or with your family. Every minute should be enjoyed and savored."

- Earl Nightingale

"*O*ur greatest happiness in life does

not depend on the condition of life in which chance has placed us, but is always the result of good conscience, good health, occupation, and freedom in all just pursuits."

- Thomas Jefferson

"*A*ction may not always bring

happiness; but there is no happiness
without action."

- Mahatma Ghandi

"*A*ct happy, feel happy, be happy,

without a reason in the world. Then you
can love, and do what you will."

- Dan Millman

"*S*uccess and happiness are not

matters of chance but choice."

- Zig Ziglar

"*T*he most wasted of all days is one
without laughter."

    - E.E. Cummings

"*T*he third-rate mind is only happy
when it is thinking with the majority.
The second-rate mind is only happy
when it is thinking with the minority.
The first-rate mind is only happy when it
is thinking."

    - A. A. Milne

"*W*e deem those happy who from the
experience of life have learned to bear its
ills, without being overcome by them."

    - Decimus Junius Juvenal

By Robyna Smith-Keys.

"*N*one is more impoverished than the

one who has no gratitude. Gratitude is a
currency that we can mint for ourselves,
and spend without fear of bankruptcy."

- Fred De Witt Van Amburgh

"*I*n the end, it's not the years in your

life that count, it's the life in your years."

- Abraham Lincoln

"*M*ake it a rule of life never to regret

and never to look back. Regret is an
appalling waste of energy; you can't
build on it; it's only for wallowing in."

- Katherine Mansfield

"*T*he sign of intelligent people is their

ability to control emotions by the
application of reason."

- Marya Mannes

" *W*hat everyone wants from life is

continuous and genuine happiness."

- Baruch Spinoza

"*A* psychologically healthy person can,

in fact, be defined as someone whose
desires actually produce happiness."

- Deepak Chopra

" *M*any people have a wrong idea of

what constitutes true happiness. It is not attained through self-gratification, but through fidelity to a worthy purpose."

- Helen Keller

" *P*leasure is not happiness. It has no

more importance than a shadow following a man."

- Muhammad Ali

" *P*atience is a necessary ingredient of

genius"

- Benjamin Disraeli

"*P*rogress in every age results only from the fact that there are some men and women who refuse to believe that what they know to be right cannot be done."

- Russell W. Davenport

"*I*t is only possible to live happily ever after on a day to day basis."

- Margaret Bonnano

"*L*ife is ten percent what happens to you and ninety percent how you respond to it."

- Lou Holtz

By Robyna Smith-Keys.

" *W*hat is the meaning of life? To be

happy and useful."

- The Dalai Lama

" *B*eing happy doesn't mean everything

is perfect. It means you have decided to
look beyond the imperfections."

- Unknown Author

" *W*hoever is happy will make others

happy, too."

- Mark Twain

"*A*n optimist sees an opportunity in

every calamity; a pessimist sees a
calamity in every opportunity."

- Winston Churchill

"*T*he world of those who are happy is

different from the world of those who
are not."

- Ludwig Wittgenstein

"*E*very day do something that will inch

you closer to a better tomorrow."

- Doug Firebaugh

357

By Robyna Smith-Keys.

"*D*ream as if you'll live forever, live as if you'll die today."

- James Dean

"*T*hink of all the beauty still left around you and be happy."

- Anne Frank

"*C*ontentment is not the fulfillment of what you want, but the realization of how much you already have."

- Author Unknown

"*T*here is only one thing that makes a

dream impossible to achieve:

the fear of failure."

- Paulo Coelho

"*T*he art of being happy lies in the

power of extracting happiness from
common things."

- Henry Ward Beecher

"*T*o be without some of the things you

want is an indispensable part of
happiness."

- Bertrand Russell

By Robyna Smith-Keys.

"*J*ust think how happy you'd be if you
lost everything and everyone you have
right now, and then, somehow got
everything back again."

- Yobi Yamada

"*T*he life that conquers is the life that
moves with a steady resolution and
persistence toward a predetermined
goal. Those who succeed are those who
have thoroughly learned the immense
importance of a plan in life, and the
tragic brevity of time."

- W.J. Davison

"*T*he road to happiness lies in two simple principles: find what it is that interests you and that you can do well, and when you find it, put your whole soul into it -- every bit of energy and ambition and natural ability you have."

- John D. Rockefeller III

"*S*ometimes it's important to work for that pot of gold. But other times it's essential to take time off and to make sure that your most important decision in the day simply consists of choosing which color to slide down on the rainbow."-

- Douglas Pagels

By Robyna Smith-Keys.

These Are the Gifts I'd Like to Give to You

"There are two things to aim at in life; first to get what you want, and after that to enjoy it. Only the wisest of mankind has achieved the second".

- Logan Pearsall Smith

"It's good to have money and the

things that money can buy, but it's good, too, to check up once in a while and make sure that you haven't lost the things that money can't buy."

- George Horace Lorimer

"*T*he mind is its own place, and in itself, can make heaven of Hell, and a hell of Heaven."

- John Milton

"*H*appiness comes from counting our blessings, appreciating little things – a flower by a stream, seagulls circling over the ocean, laughter of little children, a call from a friend, a challenge met. Happiness comes from celebrating the moment - not waiting for all our problems to be solved. Happiness comes from cultivating a thankful heart."

- Author Unknown

By Robyna Smith-Keys.

" *O*ptimism is the one quality more
associated with success and happiness
than any other."

- Brian Tracy

" *W*hen one door of happiness closes,
another opens; but often we look so long
at the closed door that we do not see the
one which has been opened for us."

- Helen Keller

"*T*he truest greatness lies in being
kind, the truest wisdom in a happy
mind."

- Ella Wheeler Wilcox

"*In* times of great stress or adversity,

it's always best to keep busy, to plow
your anger and your energy into
something positive".

- Lee Iacocca

"*Those* who bring sunshine into the

lives of others, cannot keep it from
themselves."

- James M. Barrie

"*It* is not in doing what you like, but in

liking what you do that is the secret of
happiness."

- James M. Barrie

By Robyna Smith-Keys.

"*T*here is nothing more attractive than

a happy person."

- Author Unknown

"*H*appiness often sneaks in through a

door you didn't know you left open."

- John Barrymore

"*T*he true way to render ourselves

happy is to love our work and find in it
our pleasure."

- Francoise de Motteville

"*A*ll seasons are beautiful for the person who carries happiness within."

- Horace Friess

"*T*he basic thing that everyone wants is happiness, no one wants suffering. And happiness mainly comes from our own attitude, rather than from external factors. If your own mental attitude is correct, even if you remain in a hostile atmosphere, you feel happy."

- The Dalai Lama

"*H*appiness belongs to the self-sufficient"

- Aristotle

By Robyna Smith-Keys.

" *The* happiness that is genuinely

satisfying is accompanied by the fullest
exercise of our faculties and the fullest
realization of the world in which we
live."

- Bertrand Russell

" *G*ratefulness is the key to a happy life

that we hold in our hands, because if we
are not grateful, then no matter how
much we have we will not be happy --
because we will always want to have
something else or something more."

- Brother David Steindl-Rast

"*Y*ou can never get enough of what you

don't need to make you happy."

            - Eric Hoffer

"*B*eing happy doesn't mean that
everything is perfect. It means that
you've decided to look beyond the
imperfections."

            - Author Unknown

"*I* don't know what your destiny will

be, but one thing I do know: the only
ones among you who will be really
happy are those who have sought and
found how to serve."

            - Albert Schweitzer

By Robyna Smith-Keys.

"*H*appiness is the meaning and the

purpose of life, the whole aim and end of
human existence"

- Aristotle

"*T*he Grand essentials of happiness

are: something to do, something to love,
and something to hope for."

Allan K. Chalmers

"*H*appiness comes when your work and words are of benefit to yourself and others."

- Buddha

"*H*appiness consists more in small conveniences or pleasures that occur every day, than in great pieces of good fortune that happen but seldom in life"

- Ben Franklin

"*P*eople need hard times and oppression to develop psychic muscles."

- Emily Dickinson

371

By Robyna Smith-Keys.

"*N*one is more impoverished than the

one who has no gratitude. Gratitude is a currency that we can mint for ourselves, and spend without fear of bankruptcy"

- Fred De Witt Van Amburgh

"*A* thankful heart is not only the

greatest virtue, but the parent of all the other virtues"

- Cicero (Marcus Tullius Cicero)

"*H*appiness and misery depend not

upon how high up or how low down you are – but on the direction in which you are tending"

-Samuel Butler

"*T*he greatest glory is not in never failing, but in rising up every time we fall."

- Confucius

"*H*e is a man of sense who does not grieve for what he has not, but rejoices in what he has."

- Epictetus

"*W*e make a living by what we get, but we make a life by what we give."

- Norman MacFinan

By Robyna Smith-Keys.

"*B*elieve in yourself! Have faith in your

abilities! Without a humble but
reasonable confidence in your own
powers you cannot be

successful or happy."

- Norman Vincent Peale

" *W*orry never robs tomorrow of its

sorrow; it just saps the joy out of today."

- Leo Buscaglia

"*The* road to happiness lies in two

simple principles: find what it is that
interests you and that you can do well,
and when you find it, put your whole
soul into it -- every bit of energy and
ambition and natural ability you have."

- John D. Rockefeller III

"*What* a man is contributes much

more to his happiness than what he has,
or how he is regarded by others."

- Arthur Schopenhauer

By Robyna Smith-Keys.

" **R**eflect upon your present blessings,

of which every man has many - not on your past misfortunes, of which all men have some."

- Charles Dickens

" **O**ne day in retrospect the years of

struggle will strike you as the most beautiful."

- Sigmund Freud

" **T**he habit of giving only enhances the

desire to give."

- Walt Whitman

"*I* believe life is constantly testing us for our level of commitment, and life's greatest rewards are reserved for those who demonstrate a never-ending commitment to act until they achieve. This level of resolve can move mountains, but it must be constant and consistent. As simplistic as this may sound, it is still the common denominator separating those who live their dreams from those who live in regret."

- Anthony Robbins

"*W*ho is the happiest of men? He who values the merits of others, and in their pleasure takes joy, even as though t'were his own."

- Johann von Goethe

By Robyna Smith-Keys.

"*L*ive your life each day as you would

climb a mountain. An occasional glance
towards the summit keeps the goal in
mind, but many beautiful scenes are to
be observed from each new vantage
point."

- Harold B. Melchart

"*I*t makes no difference how many

peaks you reach if there was no pleasure
in the climb."

- Oprah

"*M*any men owe the grandeur of their

lives to their tremendous difficulties."

- Spurgeon

" *O*ur lives improve only when we take

chances - and the first and most difficult risk we can take is to be honest with ourselves."

- Walter Anderson

" *O*ur greatest happiness in life does

not depend on the condition of life in which chance has placed us, but is always the result of good conscience, good health, occupation, and freedom in all just pursuits."

- Thomas Jefferson

By Robyna Smith-Keys.

" *H*appiness cannot be traveled to,

owned, earned, worn or consumed.
Happiness is the spiritual experience

of living every minute with love, grace,
and gratitude."

- Denis Waitley

" *H*appiness gives us the energy which

is the basis for health."

- Henri Amiel

" *I*f you can give your son or daughter

only one gift, let it be enthusiasm."

- Bruce Barton

" *W*e don't always know what makes us happy. We know, instead, what we think SHOULD. We are baffled and confused when our attempts at happiness fail...We are mute when it comes to naming accurately our own preferences, delights, gifts, talents. The voice of our original self is often muffled, overwhelmed, even strangled, by the voices of other people's expectations. The tongue of the original self is the language of the heart."

- Julie Cameron

By Robyna Smith-Keys.

$\mathcal{H}$appiness Lies In

The Joy Of Achievement:

Happiness is a byproduct. You cannot pursue it by itself. You were built to conquer your environment, solve problems, and achieve goals. You'll find no real satisfaction or happiness in life without obstacles to conquer and goals to achieve. Happiness is in activity. It's a running river not a stagnant pond. Happiness is not in having or being, it's in doing something you love. The secret of happiness is in having something to do. "Regret for the things we did can be tempered by time; it is regret for the things we did not do that is inconsolable."

- Sydney J. Harris

"*B*ecome a possibilitarian. No matter

how dark things seem to be or actually are, raise your sights and see the possibilities - always see them, for they are always there."

- Norman Vincent Peale

"*T*he happy people are those who are

producing something; the bored people are those who are consuming much and producing nothing."

- William Ralph Inge

By Robyna Smith-Keys.

"*In* between stimulus and response is

a space. In that space lies our power and
freedom to choose. How we wield those
choices determines our happiness."

- Steven R. Covey

" *We* each have all the time there is;

our mental and moral status is
determined by what we do with it."

- Mary Blake

" *When* someone is happy, positive,

upbeat and passionate about things, it
trickles down."

- Andrew Jacob Mahr

"*L*et us not bankrupt our today's by

paying interest on the regrets of
yesterday and by borrowing in advance
the troubles of tomorrow."

- Ralph W. Sockman

"*H*appiness is neither virtue nor

pleasure, not this thing nor that, but
simply growth."

- W.B.Yeats

"*It* isn't the big pleasures that count

the most; it's making a great deal out of
the little ones."

- Jean Webster

By Robyna Smith-Keys.

"**W**hen guilt rears its ugly head

confront it, discuss it and let it go. The past is over. It is time to ask what can we do right, not what did we do wrong. Forgive yourself and move on."

- Bernie S. Siegel

"**I** have made it a rule of my life never

to regret and never to look back. Regret is an appalling waste of energy ... you can't build on it; it's only good for wallowing in."

- Katherine Mansfield

A parent needs to be a childs guiding
light. The one to set examples of speech,
behavior, charm, voice inflections and
effective communication. A child should
be, permitted to voice their opinion and
have their opinion validated as a point of
view and then corrected fairly. A parent
needs to walk their talk, be consistent,
set rules and follow up. Have a checking
system in place. Be of good morals and
teach empathy, decency, civility,
politeness, tidiness, helpfulness, time
management skills and money
management skills. Not all children will
grasp these skills but it is a parents
obligation to lean and teach.

-Robyna Keys-Smith

By Robyna Smith-Keys.

CHILDREN LEARN WHAT THEY LIVE

- By Dorothy Law Nolte

If a child lives with criticism,

he learns to condemn.

If a child lives with hostility,

he learns to fight.

If a child lives with fear,

he learns to be apprehensive.

If a child lives with pity,

he learns to feel sorry for himself.

If a child lives with ridicule,

he learns to be shy.

If a child lives with jealousy,

he learns what envy is.

If a child lives with shame,

he learns to feel guilty.

388

If a child lives with encouragement,

he learns to be confident.

If a child lives with tolerance,

he learns to be patient.

If a child lives with praise,

he learns to be appreciative.

If a child lives with acceptance,

he learns to love.

If a child lives with approval,

he learns to like himself.

If a child lives with recognition,

he learns that it is good to have a goal.

If a child lives with sharing,

he learns about generosity.

If a child lives with honesty and fairness,

he learns what truth and justice are.

If a child lives with security,

he learns to have faith in himself and in those about him.

By Robyna Smith-Keys.

If a child lives with friendliness,

he learns that the world is a nice place in which
to live.

If you live with serenity,

your child will live with peace of mind.

~~~ * ~~~

With what is your child living?

Do you check this list created by By Dorothy
Law Nolte; often and check your parenting
skills!?

 To have a happy household- children must
obey their parents. But they do not understand
why to obey is so important. How could they?
They have not lived through their life yet. They
need to live a life by design and consistent
instruction by consistent parents. A disorderly,
untidy, unorganized home is a dysfunctional
home. The more you do for your child the less
capable the child will be. In my next book "Are

Ba Ha Ha Happy!

You A Toxic Parent" we will analyze this more.
In the mean time learn to laugh with your
children, tickle them, create strong boundaries,
teach them to help with chores, seek help for
yourself and them. Send them to Church or Girl
Guides, Boy Scouts or Sunday School. Do not
over extend your self or their activities. They
need time with you more than they need to be
running off to after school activates.
Vacuuming and washing the car is exercise.
The fun can be in how you do it together. You
will always be a childs best toy and later their
best friend. You must be their guiding light,
their emotional balancer, their savor and most
importantly, you must be on their side.

By Robyna Smith-Keys.

TOXIC PARENTS

Dealing with toxic parents. Unfortunately, some parents are unreasonable. It could be due to their childhood experiences or the additions they took part in as teenagers and a host of other reasons.

You cannot change who they are but you can

Ba Ha Ha Happy!

change the way you deal with them. You need to leave the unraveling of their personality to a higher power. This subject like most other emotional disorders could fill a book. Here I have given a brief way for you to help yourself. I am assuming you are an adult reading this book and you are doing so to be Ba Ha ha

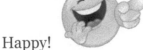

Happy!

Ba Ha Ha Happy!

When someone has been obnoxious towards me I feel like punishing them, or refusing to help them because they have been cruel to me.

But I have a talk to myself and repeat over and over; "Two Wrong Do Not Make A Right." I repeat this saying to myself over and over and remember my parents saying:-

Someone has to be in the right,

Someone has to do what is right.

Then I do what is right but I create my boundaries.

Any father / mother who could be cruel to a child is not going to apologize to that child when they've grown up. If you have been through the treadmill of living with toxic parents it is time to break the mold.

Take everything negative about your mother/ father and flip it. Dust it off.

By Robyna Smith-Keys.

1. Think & Try:-

I will create a welcoming and warm home life; I will express love and encourage others daily; I will extend myself to those in need and I will remember: a life well-lived is the best revenge.

2. Five ways to say no to my toxic mother / father:

A. No, I won't be doing that.

B. No, don't count on my being there.

C. No, I'm done subjecting myself to your drama.

D. No, I choose not to accept the stress.

E. No, I have more positive things to do.

I can tell my toxic mother / father that as I've grown into a woman (or man) I've developed a better understanding of the choices he / she made. (That should shut him / her up for a few moments).

Maneuvering your life around alcoholic or drug induced parents is a nightmare for the young. If you are under eighteen and reading this book here is a good tool for you.

Agree with everything they say, while they are in a lunatic state.

Call the kids help line or Lifeline or any other free counseling service for a chat. If you do not want to move out of home you do not need to tell the telephone councilor where you live nor your last name.

Never every try to explain to your father / mother that you did not do what they are wrongly-blaming you of while they are in a bad mood. Wait for the right moment. That could be the next morning or next week or the next decade, even longer but you will get your

By Robyna Smith-Keys.

chance. While they are intoxicated or in a bad mood your chances of them listening to you effectively are zero to naught, second to non, zilch.

Ba Ha Ha Happy!

SELF-CONTROL

How to have self-control.

Answer:

Before you think, speak, or act, in any specific way, first evaluate:

Would this be detrimental to myself, or others in any way, now, later, or much later?

If so: Don't think, speak, or act so evermore!

If not: Please continue to think, speak, or act so.

 During thinking, speaking, or acting in any specific way, then furthermore evaluate:

Would this be detrimental to others or me in any possible way, now, later, or much later?

If so: Do not think, speak, or act so evermore!

By Robyna Smith-Keys.

If not: Please continue to think, speak, or act so.

After thinking, speaking, or acting in any specific way, then finally evaluate:

Would this be detrimental to myself, or others in any possible way, now, later, or much later?

If so: Do not think, speak, or act so evermore!

If not: Please continue to think, speak, or act so.

Take-home: Before, during, and after!

- Buddha

Remind yourself:-

"Two wrongs do not make a right." Is this the right thing to say or do????

Ba Ha Ha Happy!

Affirmation

~~~~~~

To-day

Before I speak I will pause

Take a deep breath

Release my breath slowly

While I breath slowly in and out I will ask myself should I say that?

Will I cause an unfavorable reaction?

Remind yourself:-

"Two wrongs do not make a right." Is this the right thing to say or do????

By Robyna Smith-Keys.

"Two wrongs don't make a right."

"The pen is mightier than the sword."

"When in Rome, do as the Romans."

"The squeaky wheel gets the grease."

"When the going gets tough, the tough get going."

"No man is an island."

"*Fortune favors the bold.*"

"*If it aren't broke, don't fix it.*"

"*People who live in glass houses should not throw stones.*"

"*Don't criticize other people if you're not perfect yourself.*"

"*Better late than never.*"

"*Birds of a feather flock together.*"

"*Beauty is in the eye of the beholder.*"

By Robyna Smith-Keys.

"*Beggars can't be choosers.*"

"*Keep your friends close and your enemies closer.*"

"*A picture is worth a thousand words.*"

"*Hope for the best, but prepare for the worst.*"

"*Discretion is the greater part of valor.*"

"*The early bird catches the worm.*"

"*Never look a gift horse in the mouth.*"

Ba Ha Ha Happy!

"*You* can't make an omelet without breaking a few eggs."

"*God* helps those who help themselves."

"*You* can't always get what you want."

"*Cleanliness* is next to godliness."

"*A* watched pot never boils."

"*Too* many cooks spoil the broth."

"*Actions* speak louder than words."

"*Practice* makes perfect."

403

By Robyna Smith-Keys.

"*Easy come, easy go.*"

"*Don't bite the hand that feeds you.*"

"*All good things must come to an end.*"

"*If you can't beat 'em, join 'em.*"

"*One man's trash is another man's treasure.*"

"*There's no such thing as a free lunch.*"

"*There's no place like home.*"

Ba Ha Ha Happy!

"There's no time like the present."

"Necessity is the mother of invention."

"A penny saved is a penny earned."

"Familiarity breeds contempt."

"You can't judge a book by its cover."

"Take care of the cents and the dollars will follow"

"Good things come to those who wait."

"Don't put all your eggs in one basket."

By Robyna Smith-Keys.

"*Two heads are better than one.*"

"*The grass is always greener on the other side of the hill.*"

"*Do unto others as you would have them do unto you.*"

"*A chain is only as strong as its weakest link.*"

"*Honesty is the best policy.*"

"*Absence makes the heart grow fonder.*"

"*You* can lead a horse to water, but you can't make him drink."

"*Don't* count your chickens before they hatch."

"*If* you want something done right, you have to do it yourself."

"*You* don't buy a watch dog and bark yourself"

"*A* bird in hand is better than three in the bush".

By Robyna Smith-Keys.

"Stinking drinking leads to stinking thinking".

"Easy Does It"

~~~~~~
FORGIVENESS OF SIN
~~~~~~

Throughout my life I have experienced people that know nothing of sin and the degrees of sin. The causes, of sin and the effects of sin. It has also been bought to my attention there are people that know they have sinned and never ever forgive themselves. There are also people that use other peoples past to condemn them forevermore. Those that condemn others forevermore, in this book I cannot help. Those that sin will eventually wakeup to themselves or be dammed in many ways. In this book, I am more concerned about those that want to more

Ba Ha Ha Happy!

forward and lead a better life. Those of you that do not forgive yourself can do so right now. Connect with a power greater than you. Pray to your Guardian Angel (Angel Of God) and ask God or your higher power for forgiveness. Say the prayer "Angel Of God" and "Act Of Contrition" each day.

Then trust in the fact that you are forgiven. Design your life in such a way you will never ever make the same mistakes ever again.

ANGEL OF GOD

Angel of God, my guardian dear,

to whom God's love commits me here,

ever this day be at my side,

to light and guard, to rule and guide.

Amen

By Robyna Smith-Keys.

ACT OF CONTRITION

O my God,

I am heartily sorry for having

offended Thee,

and I detest all my sins because of thy
just punishments,

but most of all because they offend Thee,

my God, who art all good and deserving
of all my love.

I firmly resolve with the help of

Thy grace

to sin no more and to avoid the near
occasion of sin.

Amen.

PHOBIAS

Phobias are irrational fears and dislikes. They stem from a childhood fear. Yes, they seem real and can cause high fever and unbalanced behavior. They are not something you should expect people to understand, they are after all your out of control fear.

Most people experience a degree of natural fear when exposed to heights, known as the fear of falling.

On the other hand, those who have little fear of such exposure are said to have a head for heights. A head for heights is advantageous for those hiking or climbing in mountainous terrain and also in certain jobs e.g. steeplejacks.

By Robyna Smith-Keys.

Acrophobia sufferers can experience a panic attack in high places and become too agitated to get themselves down safely. Approximately two percent of the general population suffers from acrophobia, with twice as many women affected as men.

A fear of heights during the first 42 years of my life prevented me from enjoying many wonderful experiences.

While in France visited the Eiffel Tower when I was forty one years of age. I made it to the very top and was able to do so by meditating before I went up and talking to myself. When I finished my meditation session at the base of the tower I then stood back, had a look and worked out how I was going to deal with this once in a lifetime experience and conquer my fears.

After making it to the top and enjoying each viewing level, I stepped out of the very narrow stairwell and walked towards the rail. With lightening speed, my head filled with all the most ridiculous scenarios. Fear filled my body and I froze.

The thought of getting back down became a nightmare. I sat down closed my eyes and meditated. If I did fall I would be dead and that is that. Well, I said to myself that's the worst thing that could happen. When I opened my eyes I observed the other people looking over the rail and talked to my self about how happy they were taking in the views. From that moment on sitting up there on that highest viewing platform I had the choice to conquer my fear so I could enjoy this once in a life time experience by accepting the worst scenario was death. To cut a long story short I view the sights up there by staying away from the edge and I used my movie camera to take in all the views without looking into the camera screen.

By Robyna Smith-Keys.

Then I sat close to the exit, did some meditation and finally made my way back down the narrow stairwell to the landing where the lift was. While sitting at a nearby cafe, I viewed what I had captured on film. The next day I went back and again went to the top. The outcome that second visit was an amazing experience. I did become a little fearful but I even looked straight down. No longer am I afraid of heights, but I still need to meditate and do some self-talk exercises.

You cannot go through life saying I am afraid of .... whatever it is you are afraid of and leave it at that. You cannot go through life and expect others to accept that is your fear. It is your duty as a human to conquer all fears and negatives in your life.

It is your responsibility to challenge yourself. Life changes for the best, when you practice being responsible. Relinquishing responsibility for improvement – is not easy. Once we stop blaming outside forces for our misfortunes or predicaments, there is only one place to look:-

The mirror!

PHOBIA LIST

~~~~~~

Achievemephobia – The fear of success. The opposite to the fear of failure.

Achondroplasiaphobia – The fear of midgets. Because they look differently.

Acrophobia – The fear of heights. Five percent of the general population suffer from this phobia.

Aerophobia – The fear of flying. 25 million Americans share a fear of flying.

Agliophobia – The fear of pain. Being afraid something painful will happen.

By Robyna Smith-Keys.

Agoraphobia – The fear of open or crowded spaces. People with this fear often wont leave home.

Ailurophobia – The fear of cats. This phobia is also known as Gatophobia.

Alektorophobia – The fear of chickens. You may have this phobia if chickens make you panic.

Allodoxaphobia – The fear of opinions. Being afraid of hearing what others are thinking of you.

Anatidaephobia – The fear of ducks. Somewhere, a duck is watching you.

Androphobia – The fear of men. Usually seen in younger females, but it can also affect adults.

Anthropophobia – The fear of people. Being afraid of people in all situations.

Aphenphosmphobia – The fear of intimacy. Fear of being touched and love.

Apiphobia – The fear of bees. Many people fear being stung by angry bees.

Aquaphobia – The fear of water. Being afraid of water or being near water.

Arachnophobia – The fear of spiders affects women four times more (48% women and 12% men).

Astraphobia – The fear of thunder/lightning AKA Brontophobia, Tonitrophobia, Ceraunophobia.

Athazagoraphobia – The fear of being forgotten or not remembering things.

Atychiphobia – The fear of failure. It is the single greatest barrier to success.

Autophobia – The fear of abandonment and being abandoned by someone.

By Robyna Smith-Keys.

Bananaphobia – The fear of bananas. If you have this phobia, they are scary.

Basiphobia – The fear of falling. Some may even refuse to walk or stand up.

Bathophobia – The fear of depths can be anything associated with depth (lakes, tunnels, caves).

Cacomorphobia – The fear of fat people. Induced by the media. Affects some anorexics/bulimics.

Carcinophobia – The fear of cancer. People with this develop extreme diets.

Catoptrophobia – The fear of mirrors. Being afraid of what you might see.

Chaetophobia – The fear of hair. Phobics tend to be afraid of other peoples hair.

Chronophobia – The fear of the future. A persistent fear of what is to come.

418

Cibophobia – The fear of food. The phobia may come from a bad episode while eating, like choking.

Claustrophobia – The fear of small spaces like elevators, small rooms and other enclosed spaces.

Coasterphobia – The fear of roller coasters. Ever seen Final Destination 3?

Coulrophobia – The fear of clowns. Some people find clowns funny, coulrophobics certainly don't.

Cynophobia – The fear of dogs. This includes everything from small Poodles to large Great Danes.

Didaskaleinophobia – The fear of school. This phobia affects kids mostly.

Disposophobia – The fear of getting rid of stuff triggers extreme hoarding.

By Robyna Smith-Keys.

Emetophobia – The fear of vomiting and the fear of loss of your self control.

Enochlophobia – The fear of crowds is closely related to Ochlophobia and Demophobia. Trypanophobia

Entomophobia – The fear of bugs and insects, also related to Acarophobia.

Equinophobia – The fear of horses. Animal phobias are pretty common, especially for women.

Ergophobia – The fear of work. Often due to social or performance anxiety.

Galeophobia – The fear of sharks in the ocean or even in swimming pools.

Gamophobia – The fear of commitment or sticking with someone to the end.

Gephyrophobia – The fear of bridges and crossing even the smallest bridge.

Gerascophobia – The fear of getting old. Aging is the most natural thing, yet many of us fear it.

Globophobia – The fear of balloons. They should be fun, but not for phobics.

Glossophobia – The fear of public speaking. Not being able to do speeches.

Gynophobia – The fear of women. May occur if you have unresolved mother issues.

Hemophobia – The fear of blood. Even the sight of blood can cause fainting.

Hippopotomonstrosesquippedaliophobia – The fear of long words. Pronunciation- Hippo poto monstrose quiped alio phobi

Homophobic - Disapproval, or fear of gay and lesbian people

Iatrophobia – The fear of doctors. Do you delay doctor visits? You may have this.

By Robyna Smith-Keys.

Ichthyophobia – The fear of fish. Includes small, large, dead and living fish.

Katsaridaphobia – The fear of cockroaches. This can easily lead to an excessive cleaning disorder.

Kinemortophobia – The fear of zombies. Being afraid that zombies attack and turn you into them.

Koumpounophobia – The fear of buttons. Clothes with buttons are avoided.

Lepidopterophobia – The fear of butterflies and often most winged insects.

Ligyrophobia – The fear of loud noises. More than the instinctive noise fear.

Metathesiophobia – The fear of change. Sometimes change is a good thing.

Monophobia – The fear of being alone. Even while eating and/or sleeping.

Ba Ha Ha Happy!

Mottephobia – The fear of moths. These insects are only beautiful to some.

Musophobia – The fear of mice. Some people find mice cute, but phobics don't. Catoptrophobia

Myrmecophobia – The fear of ants. Not as common as Arachnophobia, but may feel just as intense.

Mysophobia – The fear of germs. It is also rightly termed as Germophobia or Bacterophobia, Trypophobia

Misogynists - A mans fear and dislike of women.

Nosocomephobia – The fear of hospitals. Let's face it, no one likes hospitals.

Numerophobia – The fear of numbers and the mere thought of calculations.

By Robyna Smith-Keys.

Nyctophobia – The fear of darkness. Being afraid of the dark or the night is common for kids.

Ombrophobia – The fear of rain. Many fear the rain due to stormy weather.

Omphalophobia – The fear of belly buttons. Touching and looking at navels.

Ophidiophobia – The fear of snakes. Phobics avoid certain cities because they have more snakes.

Ornithophobia – The fear of birds. Individuals suffering from this may only fear certain species.

Panophobia – The fear of everything or fear that terrible things will happen.

Paraskevidekatriaphobia – The fear of Friday the 13th. About 8% of Americans have this phobia.

Pediophobia – The fear of dolls. This phobia could well be Chucky-induced.

Phasmophobia – The fear of ghosts. AKA Spectrophobia.

Philophobia – The fear of love. Being scared of falling in love or emotional commitment.

Phobophobia – The fear of fear. The thought of being afraid of objects / situations.

Photophobia – The fear of light caused by something medical or traumatic.

Podophobia – The fear of feet. Some people fear touching or looking at feet, even their own.

Pogonophobia – The fear of beards or being scared of/around bearded men.

Pseudodysphagia – The fear of choking often after a bad eating experience.

By Robyna Smith-Keys.

Pyrophobia – The fear of fire. A natural/primal fear that can be debilitating.

Ranidaphobia – The fear of frogs. Often caused by episodes from childhood.

Samhainophobia – The fear of Halloween affects children/superstitious people. Samhainophobia

Scelerophobia – The fear of crime involves being afraid of burglars, attackers or crime in general.

Scoleciphobia – The fear of worms. Often because of unhygienic conditions.

Sidonglobophobia – The fear of cotton balls or plastic foams. Oh that sound.

Somniphobia – The fear of sleep. Being terrified of what might happen right after you fall asleep.

Ba Ha Ha Happy!

Spheksophobia – The fear of wasps. You panic and fear getting stung by it.

Taphophobia – The fear of being buried alive by mistake and waking up in a coffin underground.

Technophobia – The fear of technology is often induced by culture/religion.

Telephonophobia – The fear of talking on the phone. Phobics prefer texting.

Thalassophobia – The fear of the ocean. Water, waves and unknown spaces.

Thanatophobia – The fear of death. Even talking about death can be hard.

Theophobia – The fear of God causes an irrational fear of God or religion.

Tokophobia – The fear of pregnancy involves giving birth or having children.

By Robyna Smith-Keys.

Triskaidekaphobia – The fear of the number 13 or the bad luck that follows.

Trypanophobia – The fear of needles. I used to fear needles (that and death).

Trypophobia – The fear of holes is an unusual but pretty common phobia.

Vehophobia – The fear of driving. This phobia affects personal and work life.

Xenophobia – The fear of the unknown. Fearing anything or anyone that is strange or foreign. Achievemephobia

Zoophobia – The fear of animals. Applies to both vile and harmless animals.

OTHER BOOKS BY ROBYNA SMITH-KEYS

HEALING AND TRAINING MANUALS

FOOLPROOF AROMATHERAPY

Essential oils can heal, sooth and energize. Learn how to mix. When not to use and all the benefits for hundreds of ailments listed in alphabetical order. A user friendly style of training manual.

ORGANIC CANCER CURE

A brief description on how we gave my mother back her quality of time after she had been told she only has a few days to live. We gave mum a few more years and restored her health and

By Robyna Smith-Keys.

energy with raw beetroot, turmeric and pepper. As well as Tasmanian lavender oil. This book is free on my website and with most major eBook sales companies.

ORGANIC SKINCARE RECIPES

How to have a glowing complexion and how to make the skincare at home.

THE ANTIQUE HEALER

This is a much large Aromatherapy book with photos and more healings. Also contains wise old women's remedies.

I WAS NOT READY TO LOSE MY MOTHER

My mother had a few weeks to live. Her Cancer was very aggressive. I set her up on a healing program of juices, essential oils and herbs. This was all working until she stopped the program. It also has a lovely storey about her life.

Ba Ha Ha Happy!

Married at age 16 until her Passover at 83 years of age.

HOW TO TRAINING MANUALS.

〰〰〰〰〰〰〰〰〰〰〰〰〰〰〰〰〰〰〰〰〰

BODY PIERCING BASICS

All the main points on body piercing.

BODY PIERCING FOR STUDENTS

All the main points on body piercing with forms and piercing tray setups.

ANATOMY FOR BODY PIERCERS

All Body Piercers should understand the body and how it works this is a wonderful tool for any Body Piercer.

By Robyna Smith-Keys.

Eyelash Grafting Training Manual

Step by step instructions with video tutorials.

Eyebrows Shaping And Tinting To Suit Face Shapes

Step by step instructions with video tutorials on eyebrow shaping, eyelash and brow tinting.

Cosmetic Tattoo Permanent Makeup Micro-pigmentation

A Training Manual with step by step training instructions. You could actually teach yourself the trade as this book is so well written.

An Angel For Cosmetic Tattooists

A helping hand for a cosmetic tattooist.

Ba Ha Ha Happy!

HAIR EXTENSIONS TRAINING MANUAL

Learn to create hair wefts, weaves, braids, wax in, and clip in Hair Extensions. There are videos to watch in the eBook.

DOG CARE AND DIY ORGANIC MEDICATION

How to take care of your dog when you cannot afford a Vet

This book also cover homemade cures for worms fleas and more..

SUPERNATURAL BOOKS:-

POSITIVE SPIRITUAL AFFIRMATIONS

Small to the point Verses to keep you thinking in a positive way.

By Robyna Smith-Keys.

MIND BLOSSOMS

How to meditate do spiritual cleansing and visualizations.

SPELLS AND RITUALS

A great Folklore book on how to do some positive Affirmations also called spells.

TAROT SCROLLS

Ask a question open a page and an inspiring answer will be there for you to read.

CHILDREN'S BOOKS:-

ROMEO AND JULIETTE KEEP MARK ANTONY

A wonderful storey about a puppy born on a boat. His white, cute and fluffy. True storey with a dash of magic added.

Ba Ha Ha Happy!

MARK ANTONY MARRIES LIZY AND HAS PUPPIES

This children good night story is loaded with photos of all the dogs and the new born puppies. A true story with a dash of fantasy added.

CONNECT WITH ROBYNA:-

Facebook:

http://www.facebook.com/robynasmithkeys

or

https://www.facebook.com/AromatherapyAndBeautySchoolBooks/

Twitter:

https://twitter.com/AuthorRobyna

By Robyna Smith-Keys.

From the day you were conceived your life was growing with all its trials and tribulations. Where you were born, to whom you were born or by whom your guardians were. Plus, many more circumstances and happenings surrounding your parents and you have molded you. Do you need to break the mold or adjust its shape?

The decision is yours and only yours.

Shape your life wisely as best you can under the conditions of your country and personal circumstances.

Marriage protects love and the growing family, the sanctuary of life. Chose your partner wisely or stay single. But a bad choice is a growing tool not an incurable disease.